THE DARWINS OF SHREWSBURY

THE DARWINS OF SHREWSBURY

ANDREW PATTISON

The History Press

First published 2009

Reprinted 2009, 2017

The History Press
The Mill, Brimscombe Port
Stroud, Gloucestershire, GL5 2QG
www.thehistorypress.co.uk

British Library Cataloguing in Publication Data.
A catalogue record for this book is available from the British Library.

ISBN 978 0 7524 4867 1

Typesetting and origination by The History Press

CONTENTS

ACKNOWLEDGMENTS

I would like to express my thanks to the following for their help with this book:

Martin Charlesworth and Adrian Burns suggested the idea, and have encouraged me along the way. Martin also kindly let me use his extensive library. The late Michael Charlesworth gave me much help with the material on Shrewsbury School. Professor Hugh Torrens alerted me to the material he had collected on the Shropshire Enlightenment. Peter Boyd located it for me and gave me access to it. Peter also helped with the images from the Shrewsbury Museum. Peter Barton provided background information on the Mytton family. Jon Bryan drew the family trees and assisted me to interpret some of the legal documents. Giles Madin helped with the illustrations. The staff at a number of different libraries and archives (The University of Wales, Llandrindod Wells, Cambridge University, Lichfield, Birmingham, Stafford, and especially Shropshire) always treated me with helpfulness and patience. The sources of the illustrations are detailed elsewhere – I am very grateful to all those mentioned for allowing me to use their material.

I owe two more people a particular debt of gratitude:

The first is Dr Richard Moore, whose knowledge of the history of medicine in Shropshire is unequalled, and which he freely shared. Richard also read the whole manuscript, and his suggestions have improved the book enormously. My second special thanks go to Lois, my wife. She has read the whole book at least twice, and made countless suggestions for improvement. She has also been a constant source of encouragement, allowing me to postpone many things that should have been done long ago.

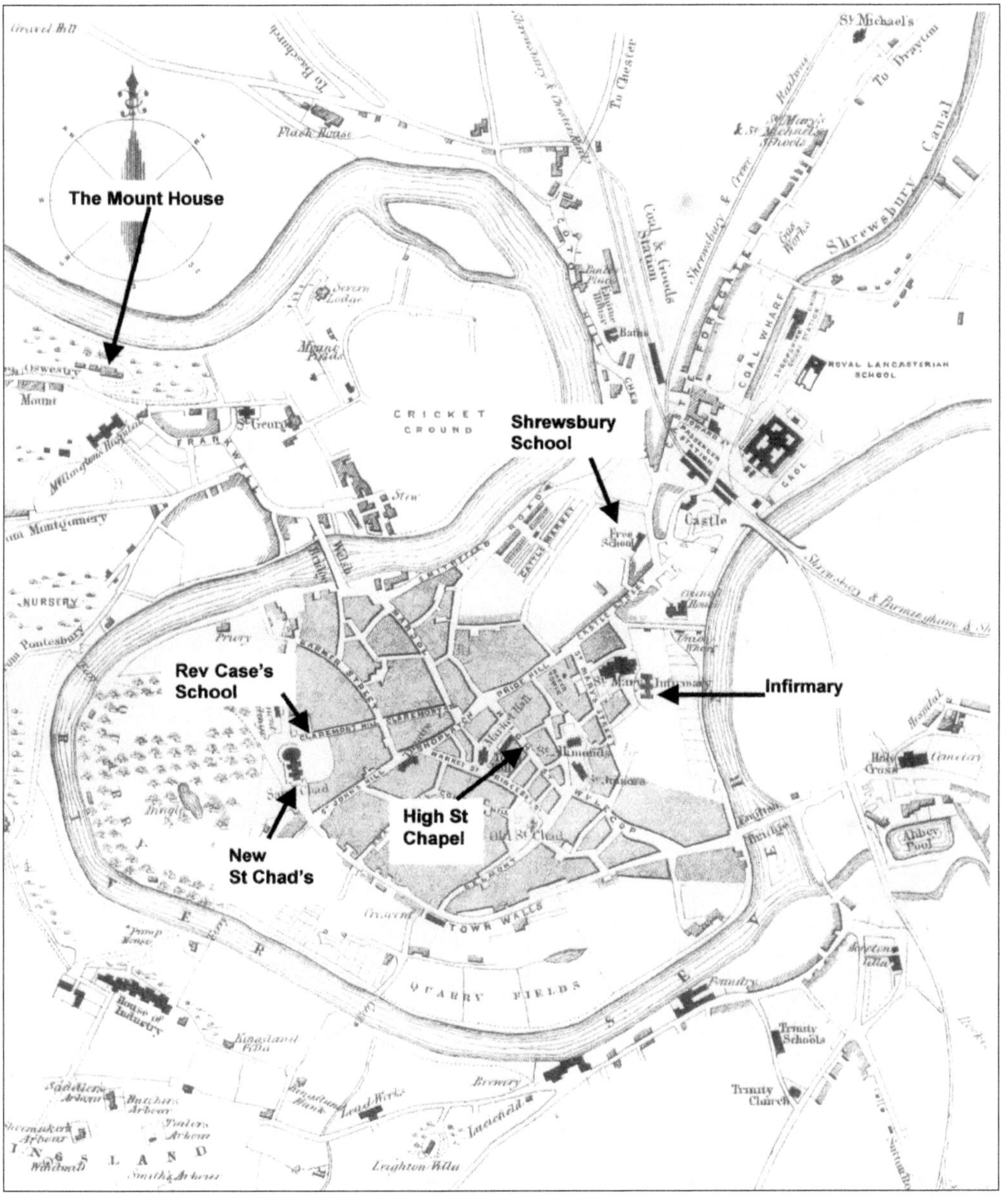

A map of Shrewsbury, *c.* 1850, showing places significant to the Darwins. (Henry Pidgeon, *Memorials of Shrewsbury* J.H. Leake, Shrewsbury, 1850)

A Concise Darwin Family Tree

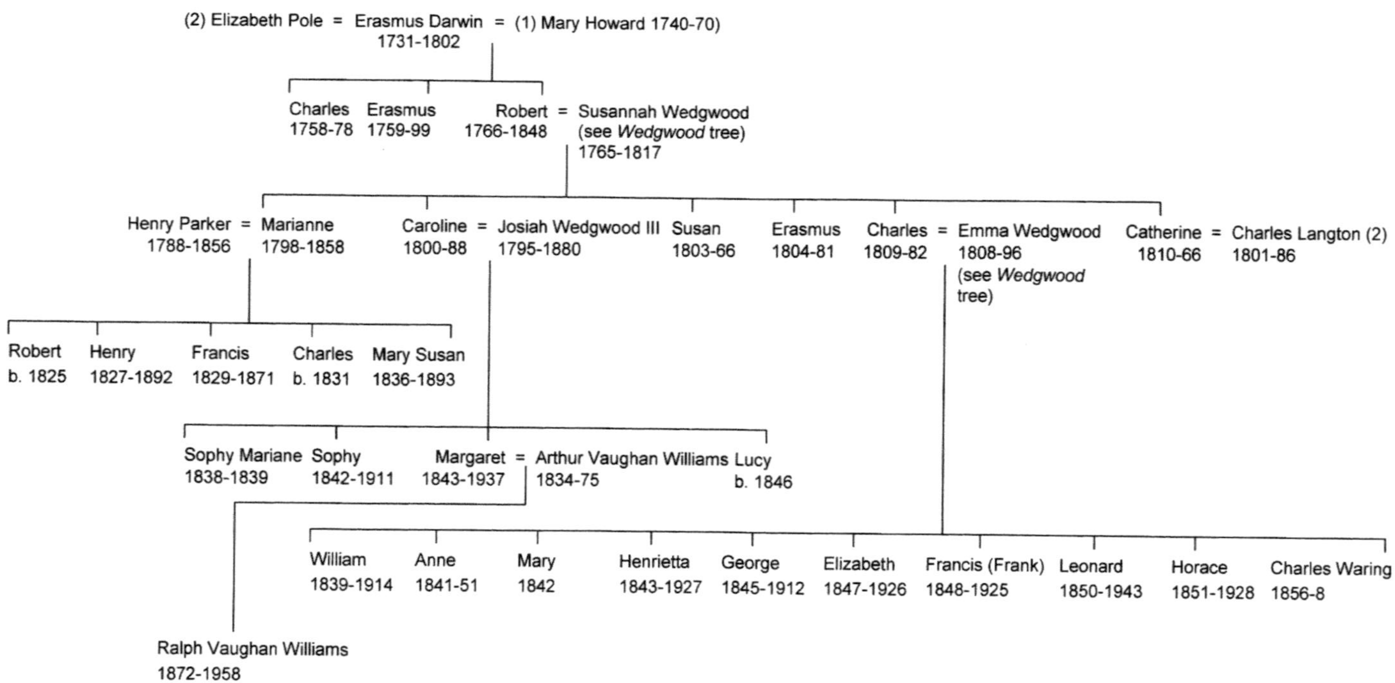

A Concise Wedgwood Family Tree

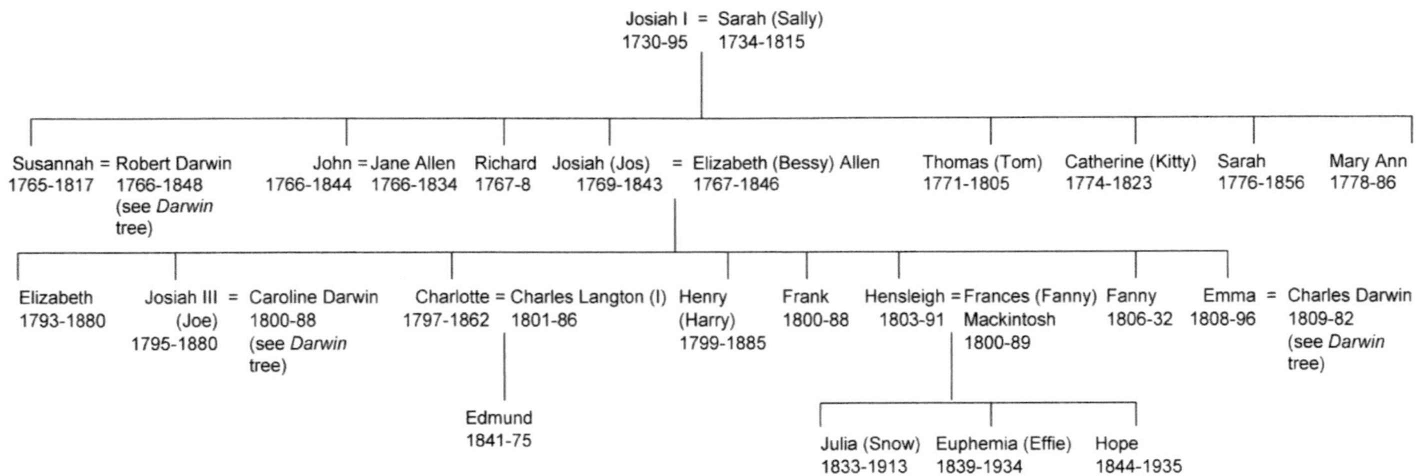

PROLOGUE

As Robert and Susannah[1] Darwin looked from their house on The Mount, high above Shrewsbury, early in February 1809, a dismal sight was spread before them. The ancient county town owes its location to its position on the River Severn, which almost encircles the low hill on which most of the town is built, but with this good defensive position comes a great disadvantage – a liability to flooding. This is exactly what occurred on the last weekend of January 1809. Swollen by melting snow from the Welsh mountains, the river reached a height not attained for fourteen years, and flooded the riverside suburbs of Frankwell, just below The Mount, and Coleham.

Robert could see that there was no way that he could get through Frankwell and over the Welsh Bridge to visit his patients in the town. He would have to wait until the water receded, unlike the Holyhead coach, whose route went past their house. At the height of the floods, the coach, which should have left at 4 a.m., eventually departed at noon. Having crossed the Welsh Bridge, the passengers had to be taken off and ferried through the streets of Frankwell by boat, leaving the poor horses (and presumably the coachman) to swim, pulling the coach with them.

Susannah shivered as she imagined what it was like for the poor families who were suddenly caught up by the floods. The local paper described their sufferings in its columns the next week. 'The fears and anguish of many poor families living in confined alleys was incalculable,' the reporter wrote, adding that 'mothers with shrieking babies were removed to places of safety.'[2] Unlike the inhabitants of Frankwell, the Darwins' home was warm and comfortable. The house reflected the family's wealth and status, its special feature being a collection of fine Wedgwood china, since Susannah was the daughter of the great Josiah Wedgwood.

The floods were not the only reason for gloom in the town. The war against Napoleon in Spain was not going well, and the retreat of the British forces, followed by the death of Sir John Moore at Corunna, had just been reported. 'Disaster upon disaster seems to be crouding [sic] upon us,' lamented the newspaper. 'We have retreated from Spain, and now have to announce the evacuation of Portugal,' the writer went on.[3] No wonder the editor urged his readers to support a day 'of general fasting and humiliation' on Wednesday 8 February, for 'never was there a crisis that called more loudly for inward humiliation and gratitude from us – as individuals, as a community, and as a nation.'[4] The war was also bringing soaring inflation. For example, the

A view of Shrewsbury from the west, artist and date unknown. (Shrewsbury Museums Service)

cost of wool had almost doubled, a coat that the month before had cost £3 16s was now being sold for 7 guineas.[5]

Robert and Susannah had their own anxieties as well, since the birth of their fifth child was due any day. This pregnancy had been unexpected, and it was nearly five years since their last child was born. Susannah had been seriously ill during her second and third pregnancies, and they also couldn't help remembering Mary Ann. She was Susannah's youngest sister, and was born when their mother was forty-four, the same age as Susannah now was. Exactly what was wrong with Mary Ann no one ever told Susannah and her siblings, but she never walked properly and had died at the age of eight.

In the end, Robert and Susannah's fears were groundless, and a normal Charles Robert Darwin made his appearance on Sunday 12 February 1809. He was called Charles after Robert's oldest brother, who had died of an infection contracted during an anatomical dissection while he was a medical student.

As spirits lifted in the Darwin family following Charles' safe arrival, the town also began to feel more optimistic. Gradually the floodwaters retreated, and a special fund was set up for the relief of the poor. Among the many contributors was Robert Darwin, who gave two guineas.[6] The news from Spain was better, too, as it was recognised that the diversion operated by Sir John Moore had enabled the Spanish generals to reorganise their armies and regain some territory. And even though France had taken Madrid, there was only a small French garrison in the city, and 6,000 wounded French troops were in the hospitals. The newspaper had also heard rumours of a split between France and Russia, and that Russia and Austria might declare war on France. There was even talk of possible French retreat from Spain and Portugal. Amongst some naval successes, the sloop HMS *Beagle* had captured a French privateer.[7] Little did the Darwins know what a profound influence that ship would later have on the life of their newborn son.

Fireplace in the room in which Charles Darwin was born. (Author's collection)

On 17 February the newspaper reported that the sermon text used by Revd Edward Bather at the Darwin's parish church, St Chad's, on the day of Charles' birth was, 'My people are destroyed for want of knowledge' (Hosea 4, verse 6). The aim of the sermon was to raise money for the Girls' Sunday School in the parish, and the sermon must have been a good one, because the collection amounted to £55 8s 0d, equivalent to the annual wage of a skilled craftsman. Revd Bather said that 'knowledge' is to know our moral and religious duties, and the best way of attaining knowledge is by searching the scriptures. He urged his congregation to teach the poor when they were young, since youth 'is the only season the labouring classes can spare from their daily occupations'.[8] The pursuit of knowledge (though his family did not all share the same definition of the word as Revd Bather) was also part of Charles Darwin's heritage. The Darwins also shared with the churchman a commitment to education for all.

So even if the weather was gloomy, the outlook was bright for the new addition to the Darwin family. Extraordinary ancestors, economic advantage, a commitment to learning and a desire to serve others were all part of his inheritance and upbringing. His immediate family, too, would be very important in his development. As a modern follower of Darwin has put it, 'great thinkers [like Charles Darwin] cannot be divorced from their social background'.[9]

1

THE YOUNG DOCTOR

Robert Waring Darwin was born on 30 May 1766, the third son of Erasmus Darwin (1731-1802) and his first wife Polly. Erasmus was a true polymath, who practised all his life as a doctor, first in Lichfield and later in Derby. He also had an extraordinarily original mind, and invented a vast array of objects. He was an important member of the Birmingham Lunar Circle (or Society), that did much to further scientific progress and industrial development in the Midlands. He wrote extensively on scientific subjects, especially botany, and he was also a poet of national significance, whose best-known works were *The Botanic Garden* and *The Temple of Nature*.

In matters religious Erasmus was a thoroughgoing sceptic, a product of the 'Age of Reason'. In his younger days he was much influenced by Deism, which is a view of God as 'abstract and remote; he was no longer inconvenient because he no longer encountered man with an exacting moral demand ... having "deified" nature, they "denatured" God.'[1] Erasmus was certainly one who 'deified' nature, as his poetry suggests. Having abandoned a Judeo-Christian creator-God, he wondered how the living world had come to be the way we see it. He was led back to an idea first put forward by the ancient Greeks – that all the plants and animals have developed from much simpler predecessors by a process of evolution. He took as his motto 'E Conchis Omnia' (literally 'everything from the shell'), since at that time shelled animals were thought to be the most primitive of creatures. He was criticised by the clerical establishment for these views, so tended to keep quiet on the subject for fear of losing his influential patients, but later in life he espoused evolution more openly. How much he directly influenced his grandson Charles is debatable, but 'Erasmus undoubtedly helped to produce the free-thinking climate in which his grandson formed his theories of evolution.'[2]

Erasmus was a larger than life character – tall and grossly obese, and with a marked stammer, but the speed of his thought and the dominance of his character meant he held centre stage in any gathering. His son Robert noted that he had 'a habit of making difficult subjects easy',[3] but the downside of his character was that if he was roused to anger he could become violent.

Robert had two older brothers, Charles (1758-1778) and Erasmus junior (1759-1799). Soon after Robert's birth his mother became ill, and eventually died a painful death when he was four years old.[4] It has been suggested that her death was due to the effects of alcoholism, but it is more likely that the underlying cause was gallbladder disease. She had bouts of excruciating

Erasmus Darwin, by Joseph Wright. (Reproduced courtesy of Erasmus Darwin House)

pain that she tried to palliate with alcohol, and her husband Erasmus may have unintentionally hastened her end with large doses of morphine in an effort to ease the pain. Her death had a deep effect on him, but he found it difficult to express his emotions. Soon after Polly's death, Erasmus' unmarried sister Susannah took over the running of the household, and she found a nanny for Robert – Mary Parker, who was just seventeen.

It wasn't long before Erasmus took Mary Parker as his mistress, and they had two daughters together, a fact that Erasmus took little trouble to hide. In 1781, when Robert was nearly fifteen, his father married Elizabeth Pole, a widow sixteen years his junior. She already had three children, who were slightly younger than Robert, and Erasmus and his new wife had a further seven children together, six of whom lived into adult life. Perhaps the biggest effect of these changes on Robert was that his father's time, and also his finances, were in the future spread more thinly. As soon as Robert was old enough he would need to stand on his own feet financially.

Another significant incident during Robert's childhood was the death of his eldest brother, Charles. Charles was the apple of his father's eye – energetic, intellectually brilliant and an original thinker. He had already made an impression at the Edinburgh Medical School when he died suddenly of an infection picked up in his medical studies. He was aged just twenty, and Robert was then twelve. What Robert felt about all these changes is not known, but they have been described as a 'black thread' woven into his emotional life.[5]

Erasmus Darwin's bookplate.

Part of Erasmus' coming to terms with the loss of his oldest son was to channel his medical ambitions into Robert. The choice of professions in those days was severely limited. Erasmus had no enthusiasm for either the armed forces (he hated war) or the church (as we have seen), which left just the law and medicine. Erasmus junior had already embarked on a career in the law, so Erasmus senior decided that Robert's future lay in medicine, whether the young man liked it or not.

Thus it was that on 21 January 1782, when he was not yet sixteen, Robert embarked on his medical studies.[6] First he went to London, probably to attend classes at the anatomy school run by the great John Hunter. From there Robert entered Edinburgh Medical School, like his father and brother before him. The Universities of Oxford and Cambridge were only open to members of the Church of England, and anyway were reckoned to be far behind both Edinburgh and continental universities for practical medical education. To finish his course he went to the University of Leiden in Holland in October 1784. He took his final exams in Leiden in December that year, and his MD degree was conferred on 2 February 1785.[7] The next month he moved on to Paris,[8] where he spent some time with Benjamin Franklin, an old friend of his father's. Robert was noted as a steady student with a good memory, but not brilliant or inventive like his older brother. By the end of his student days a friend of the family recorded that he was 'grown to an uncommon height [he was 6ft 2in], gay and blooming as a morn of summer.'[9] The next stage was to find a place to practise his new career.

It has been written that Robert was 'deposited in Shrewsbury in 1786 with £20 in his pocket.'[10] The truth seems to have been rather different. Robert heard that one of the doctors in Shrewsbury had recently died, so he and his brother Erasmus took a journey to Shrewsbury to see if it would be possible for Robert to set up in practice there. On the way they stayed with the Clives near Market Drayton. The great Lord Clive had been an acquaintance of their father, and Robert Clive junior, his youngest son, accompanied them to their destination. Clive wrote that, 'young Dr Darwin … is a very clever worthy young man, and I should have great pleasure in being of service to him.'[11] Robert Darwin liked what he saw in Shrewsbury, and decided to put up his plate. His father had given him £20, as had his favourite uncle. His father promised further funding if needed, saying, 'Let me know when you want more, and I will send it to you.'[12] His father also gave him a bay mare and a chestnut horse so he could make a favourable impression on his house calls.[13]

Erasmus knew exactly how to build up a successful medical practice, and he was quick to give his son advice.[14] Chiefly, he recommended 'visibility and sociability', which might be helped by dining with farmers on market days, attending social events and discreet advertising in his window. Above all, however, success would come by personal recommendations from those such as the Clives, one of the most powerful families in Shropshire. The reputation of his father would also do no harm. Another successful way of 'networking' was to join the Freemasons, which Robert did.[15] *The Shrewsbury Chronicle* recorded that 'The New Salopian Lodge of Free Masons [sic] was regularly constituted' in September 1788, when Major Charles Shereff, Deputy Provincial Grandmaster presided,[16] so Robert was presumably one of these founder members. Freemasonry was very popular at this time, and it provided a way for men of all social classes to meet on an equal footing. Thus, men of humble origins such as Thomas Telford (who, like Robert Darwin, had recently arrived in Shrewsbury), and William Hazledine, millwright turned ironmaster, could rub shoulders with gentry and landowners free from the niceties of social convention.[17] Since Freemasonry is such a secretive organisation, it is impossible to know if the Brotherhood played much of a part in Robert's later life.

By such means Robert got himself known – now he would have to earn continuing success. This he did with exceptional speed, for within six months he had taken on fifty patients, and never needed to ask his father for more money. For a twenty-year-old to succeed so quickly is remarkable – a testament to both his great personal qualities and exceptional skill as a doctor. This success came despite the fact that, certainly in the early days, he disliked his profession. Charles wrote, 'His great success as a doctor was the more remarkable, as he told me that he at first hated his profession so much that if he had been sure of the smallest pittance, or if his father had given him any choice, nothing should have induced him to follow it.'[18]

At this time Robert was under pressure from his father to further the latter's ambition for his son to become an intellectual giant. So Erasmus engineered that Robert should become a Fellow of the Royal Society like himself. To be accepted as a Fellow, Robert had to present an original paper, which he did in March 1786.[19] The paper describes what were then known as 'ocular spectra' – we now call them 'after images', which may be produced by gazing intently at a coloured patch and then closing the eyes. One can then 'see' an after image, often of a different colour from the original. The paper that Robert presented was the first description of this phenomenon. It was lively and interesting, describing the effects of different colours and speculating on how they might be produced. But did Robert write it? In all probability Erasmus had the ideas, even if Robert wrote the text. The view that Erasmus was the real author of the paper was certainly held by Charles Darwin.[20] Even though he was a Fellow of the Royal Society for the next sixty years, Robert never attended a meeting and showed no interest in its activities. However hard his father tried, he just could not make his son be like himself. Robert is often portrayed as uninspiring – it is more likely that he just single-mindedly got on with the daily round of medicine. An obituarist wrote, '[Robert Darwin] was a physician at Shrewsbury, who, although a man of considerable originality, devoted his powers almost entirely to his profession.'[21]

The practice of medicine in those days must have been exceptionally demanding. The doctor was personally responsible for his patient twenty-four hours a day, 365 days a year. It was hard to discuss problems with medical colleagues, since doctors were mostly in competition, both with their colleagues and with the host of unqualified quacks in the medical 'market place'. Sometimes, though, he would correspond with his father about difficult cases, which must have been a great help.

For example, a letter written by Erasmus to Robert in June 1790 was presumably in answer to the question, 'When does a mental patient need to be confined to a madhouse or asylum, rather than being treated at home?'[22] Erasmus' reply is astonishingly modern, touching on the diagnostic criteria for mental illness and describing common delusional ideas, such as the fear of death, hell or poverty, which Erasmus thought were probably changeable according to the culture. He then explained that these delusional ideas alone were not a reason for confinement. If confinement was considered necessary by relatives or others, the questions the doctor needed to answer were, 'Is the patient able to take care of his person and effects', and, 'Is he a danger to others?' Such advice would still hold good today.

Not surprisingly, considering the emotional pressures that they laboured under, most doctors of that time tended to be opinionated and dogmatic. This was partly to hide their ignorance, partly in the hope that, even if there was nothing else they could do, the power of suggestion might help their patient. This is well summed up by the following quotation from a contemporary of Robert Darwin's:

> It is the peculiar misfortune of the medical profession that its members can rarely dare to confess their ignorance, thinking it more or less necessary – in order to maintain their influence with their patients and with the world – to speak with equal decision, whether they are authorised by their knowledge to do so or not … [23]

This sort of dogmatism also sometimes spread into doctors' relationships with their colleagues. Obviously patients were free to consult whom they liked, but if a doctor knew that another practitioner had already been consulted, the normal etiquette was at least to inform the first doctor, or even to consult together. If the second doctor failed to do this, great animosity could be stirred up, which could even result in duels.[24] This animosity to other doctors can be seen in the young Robert Darwin, in what later became known as 'the battle of Wellington'.[25]

In September 1788 Mrs Frances Houlston, the wife of a well-known bookseller and publisher in Wellington,[26] about ten miles from Shrewsbury, became ill, probably with enteric fever. She consulted the local apothecary, Mr Cartwright, an old family friend, who then called in Robert Darwin on 19 September, who visited twice. As the patient failed to improve, Cartwright then turned to the famous Birmingham physician William Withering (1741-99), who was the son of a Wellington surgeon, and had grown up with Mrs Houlston's husband. Withering ignored the normal etiquette of the day by visiting the patient without any reference to Darwin, and, of course, changed the treatment. The patient worsened, and Withering wrote to Cartwright advising him what to do. Still she did not improve, and by 10 October her illness reached crisis point. Panicking, Cartwright consulted both doctors. Withering again replied by letter; history does not record what Darwin did. In the end it appears that Cartwright followed his own judgment, probably stopped most of the medication, and the patient recovered.

The incident led to a vitriolic exchange of correspondence between Darwin and Withering. The whole thing was probably exacerbated by the fact that there was a history of animosity between the two camps. Erasmus Darwin had got to know Withering many years before when, as a medical student, Withering spent his summers in Lichfield, where Erasmus lived and worked. Withering was later appointed physician to the infirmary at Stafford, not far from

William Withering.

Lichfield. When Dr William Small, who had a practice in Birmingham, and was a key figure in the development of the Lunar Society, died in 1775, Erasmus felt that Withering would be the ideal successor for Small's practice. Erasmus canvassed on Withering's behalf, and shortly afterwards he was appointed to the vacant practice, and also joined the Lunar Society. It did not take long for Erasmus to feel he had made a mistake, as Withering did not fit well with the Lunar group, being 'prickly and reserved'.[27] Their relationship went from bad to worse, and reached a head in 1780. The disagreement concerned who had discovered the therapeutic value of the foxglove (*digitalis*). There seems little doubt that Erasmus plagiarised Withering,[28] an expert botanist, who should be given the recognition for first having described the drug. Withering realised that very high doses of *digitalis* could be dangerous, and carefully experimented with both different preparations and different dosages. In contrast, Erasmus Darwin, in his usual 'gung-ho' manner, used doses of the foxglove leaf that were far too high, and probably killed a number of patients as a result, a fact that Withering was not slow to point out.

So the gun was primed, and went off in the hands of the unfortunate Robert Darwin. As likely as not his father put him up to it, but Robert wrote letters of complaint to Withering, which became public. He said of Withering that, 'pride dazzled your eyes and does not permit you to see your own ignorance'. He also accused Withering of being, 'a stage charlatan trying to support his declining business.'[29] In reply, Withering remarked that 'your enmity or your friendship are to me equally unimportant', and 'your letter breathes the air of impertinence'. Robert then dragged in various other cases where he felt Withering had also made mistakes as a way of demonstrating his adversary's incompetence. His father must have written this part, as it is difficult to imagine a twenty-two-year-old being aware of the personal details of past cases. Withering's reply was much more measured, as he tried to concentrate on the facts of the case.

To the neutral observer, the result of the 'pamphlet war' appears to be a stalemate, with neither doctor coming out with much credit, but in the longer term Robert Darwin seems to have won the argument, which was still remembered sixty years later. For when Robert Darwin died his obituarist noted that he had written a pamphlet 'which proved the correctness of his views, and this occasioned the visits of Dr Withering and other remote physicians to be discontinued within the range of Dr Darwin's practice.'[30]

It appears that it was not long before Robert Darwin regretted the acrimony with Withering, who would be much better remembered by posterity than either Robert or his father Erasmus. Robert's sympathies may have been aroused by the fact that, not long afterwards, Withering started to suffer from the tuberculosis that eventually killed him. In addition, Withering, like other members of the Lunar Circle, was caught up in the Birmingham riots of 1791, and narrowly escaped with his life.[31] The upshot of Robert's change of heart was that he bought up every copy of the offending pamphlet he could and burned them. Many years later the antiquarian William Phillips noticed that one of the pamphlets was up for auction. He had heard of the pamphlet, but never seen it, so he wanted it for his collection. He was surprised that another bidder was willing to pay 15s for the pamphlet, a figure Phillips could not match. Later he met Dr Darwin, who informed him that the man had been acting on his behalf, so that he could 'consign the pamphlet to the flames' with all the others.[32]

While all this was going on, in October 1788 Robert Darwin was appointed physician to the Salop Infirmary.[33] Maybe he was the only candidate, but often these positions were the subject of much lobbying and advertising in the local press, none of which happened in this case.[34] It is tempting, therefore, to assume that his father had a hand in the appointment, which, though unpaid, carried considerable prestige in the area. Opened in 1747, the Salop Infirmary was one of the first of many similar institutions up and down the country sponsored by the great and the good to provide free accommodation, nursing care and medicines for those who were unable to pay.[35] The way it worked was that a regular contribution to the finances enabled a person to sponsor or recommend patients for admission. Every Saturday was admission day, when, between the hours of 11 a.m. and noon, one of three physicians and surgeons would be on hand to examine those who presented themselves for admission. The aim of the institution

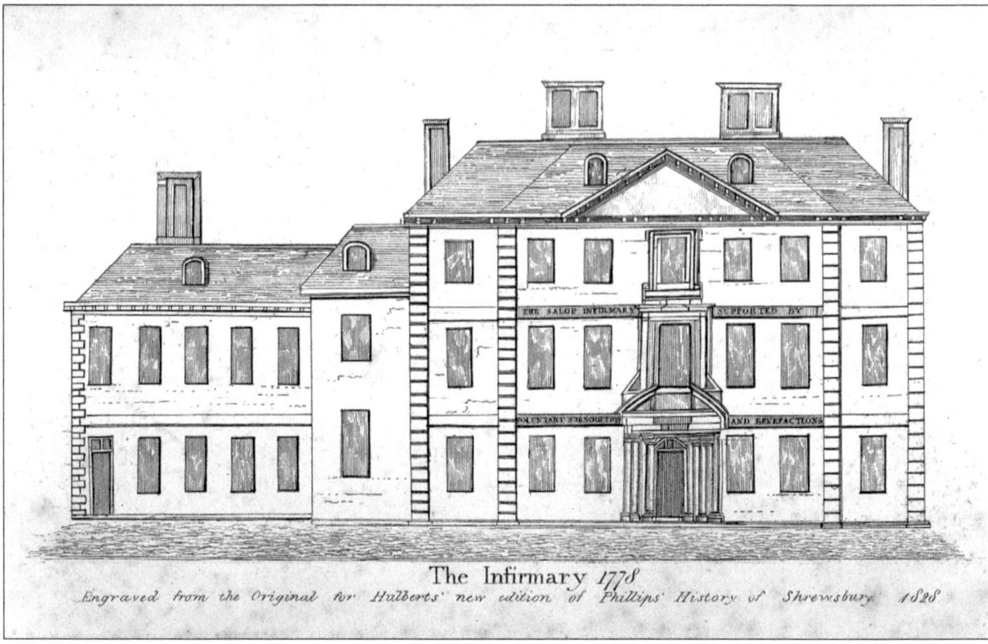

The Salop Infirmary in 1778, artist unknown. (Shrewsbury Museums Service)

was to provide proper food, rest and medicine to the 'deserving' poor who had serious, but not obviously life-threatening, illnesses. Those who could pay for their own treatment were excluded because, if admitted, the doctor would be deprived of his fees. Other potential patients who were turned away were children, those who had recurrent venereal disease and those who were obviously terminally ill. Maternity patients were also not accepted. So Robert would have to attend one Saturday in three to perform admission duties. He then passed the patients on to the resident apothecary (called the 'house surgeon' after 1792), who dealt with their routine care. The physician was required to visit and check up on them from time to time. In addition, the physicians had to examine and treat outpatients. Casualties could be admitted without prior examination at any time, and it appears that they were looked after by whichever physician or surgeon could be obtained. The bulk of inpatients were agricultural labourers and domestic servants, a reflection of the fact that the subscribers of the hospital were often their employers, and hence had a vested interest in getting them back to work as soon as possible.[36]

All in all, it was a heavy commitment for no income, so why did doctors like Robert Darwin jump at the chance of working in such an institution? A recent author sums up the benefits. She writes:

> The Salop Infirmary raised the status of the professionals and it offered educational training. Above all, it gave the professionals the time, patients, equipment and only limited interference in order to increase medical knowledge, which in turn increased their reputations.[37]

So the young doctor was firmly established on the Shrewsbury scene. He wanted to get married, but first he needed to be financially secure.

2

MONEY AND MATRIMONY

In the matter of making money, Robert Darwin was far more astute than his father. In his first ten months in practice he earned £55. The next year his income had increased to £259, and the year after that it was £520.[1] By 1791, five years after starting in practice, his income from fees was £1,180.[2] This was augmented with a legacy he inherited from his maternal grandfather's estate that was finally paid up in October 1790. This amounted to £1,137 10s 6d, and was boosted early the following year by a further £100 legacy from an uncle on his mother's side.[3] This uncle also left him £1,000 invested in the Lichfield Turnpike tolls, which would provide a steady source of income.[4] Converting to modern day monetary values is notoriously difficult, since the costs of various aspects of life inflate differently. However, by way of comparison, in 1800 a reasonably skilled worker earned around £50 a year, while a shopkeeper might earn £150. Clergymen earned from £120-500, depending on their status. At the top of the tree, peers might have an annual income of £8,000.[5] By any criteria Robert Darwin's income was exceptional.

Robert didn't waste his money on idle living, but put it to work. Thus began a lifetime of careful investments and meticulous book keeping, which was to have a profound impact on his immediate family and far beyond. Finance, rather than medicine, was what he really seemed to enjoy. The first significant investment he made was in the new St Chad's Church in Shrewsbury. The old St Chad's Church tower had collapsed in July 1788, just as Thomas Telford had predicted. Rather than repair the old church, it was decided to build a completely new one on the old town walls, at the top of the hill overlooking the Quarry Park. Building work began in 1790, but, as so often happens, costs overran, and in February 1791 the trustees had to apply to Parliament for permission to raise more funds.[6] Robert offered £1,000 to the rebuilding fund; this was not a gift, but a commercial loan with interest at 5 per cent per annum.[7] So, in addition to getting the loan back, he earned another £50 a year in interest payments. Repayment was guaranteed – church tithes would see to that.

Robert also invested his money in land and property, in deals for which his brother Erasmus acted as his solicitor. In late 1793 he bought a small estate in the Crowmere/Belvidere area on the eastern edge of Shrewsbury, where Flagwall and Barleyfields, two of the fields he bought, are remembered as street names.[8] He sold this land in August 1800,[9] making £105 profit, as well as benefiting from seven years' rental income.[10]

During this period Robert became a well-known figure in the life of the town. He may not have been an original thinker like his father, but he had an active and enquiring mind. As Charles later wrote, 'My father's mind was not scientific, and he did not try to generalise his knowledge under general laws; yet he formed a theory for almost everything which occurred.'[11] From this we see how Robert's careful, quantifiable and measured outlook and interests form a vital link between the idiosyncratic brilliance of his father Erasmus and the mixture of originality and obsession we find in his son Charles.

Robert was also a gregarious person, and boasted a group of friends of unusual energy and ability. Shrewsbury had no philosophical or scientific society until 1835, so relationships between these men were informal, but they collaborated in many ways. Many of them were industrialists, like William Reynolds of Coalbrookdale; Charles Bage, who designed the Ditherington Flax Mill, the first iron-framed building in the world; William Hazledine, the ironmaster; and Thomas Telford, the celebrated engineer. Others members of the group were Samuel Butler, headmaster of Shrewsbury School; Owen and Blakeway, the antiquarians; Archdeacon Joseph Plymley, best known as an anti-slavery campaigner; and Robert Townson, a pioneer of geology. During the 1790s and early 1800s all of these men were active in and around Shrewsbury, which was the hub of what has been described as 'The Shropshire Enlightenment.'[12, 13]

An example of how these men co-operated is shown in Joseph Plymley's book on the agriculture of Shropshire.[14] The archdeacon had been commissioned to write the book, which was one of a series on each county, published by the government to improve the agriculture of the whole country. Plymley could not be an expert on everything, so he picked his friends' brains. For this reason the book is full of references to the work of others, and reads like a 'Who's Who' of Shropshire intellectual life at the time. Thomas Telford wrote a section on canals, William Reynolds is quoted extensively, as is Robert Townson, the geological expert. Robert Darwin and Thomas DuGard (then the house surgeon at the Salop Infirmary) both get a mention in relation to water analysis.[15]

As well as their interest in improving industry, agriculture and social conditions, these men shared a similar political outlook. Political allegiances were much less clear-cut in those days, but most of the men in this group would have classed themselves as being of a liberal or Whig frame of mind. This was certainly the case with Robert Darwin at that period, but he felt it was unwise to express these opinions amongst his affluent Tory patients. His advice to a young colleague about to embark on a medical career reflected this. Robert Darwin said, 'Never marry a pretty woman, and never take part in politics.' Quite what the first part of the advice was supposed to mean the young man never did work out, but he recognised that his mentor certainly followed the second part.[16]

Another cause that Robert Darwin threw himself into was that of the abolition of the slave trade, which the Darwins and Wedgwoods began to support in about 1788.[17] In April 1791, a motion by William Wilberforce to abolish the slave trade was again defeated in Parliament,[18] and the anti-slavery lobby knew that they had to mobilise public opinion if their campaign was to succeed. The most prominent national activist was Thomas Clarkson, who travelled the country encouraging the formation of local groups. His key contact in Shropshire was Archdeacon Plymley, who advertised a meeting with the aim of setting up of a local group.[19] The meeting duly took place in the Shire Hall on 13 July 1791, with Plymley in the chair. Amongst those who attended was Robert Darwin.[20] The meeting sent a message of encouragement to their supporters in Parliament, and it also commended the labours of Thomas Clarkson and Joseph Plymley. Those present resolved to support the anti-slavery cause in any way they could, to

Archdeacon Joseph Plymley. (Charles Hulbert, *The History and Description of the County of Salop* Private Publication, 1837)

which end they printed their names and these resolutions for three weeks in the newspapers, requesting others to subscribe to the cause. Clarkson was not present at that meeting, but he subsequently made many visits to Shrewsbury, staying at the Plymley household, Longnor Hall, on the Ludlow Road.[21] What part Robert Darwin played in the local campaign we do not know, but the fact that he was willing to support a cause publicly that may have been unpopular with some of his aristocratic patients suggests a degree of moral courage.

A much less contentious cause that Robert Darwin supported was the formation of a local branch of the Humane Society. This society was founded in London in 1774 to encourage the application of the newly developed techniques of resuscitation to those who had fallen into water and appeared drowned.[22] The River Severn in Shrewsbury has a melancholy record of people drowning, and it was worse in those days than now. Few people then learned to swim, and as there were only two bridges over the river in the town many people crossed by means

Josiah Wedgwood I. (Courtesy of the Wedgwood Museum Trust, Barlaston, Staffordshire)

of coracles or other flimsy craft. The stimulus for the formation of the society appears to have been the case of one Jacky Sandford, a well-known local character, who fell in the river one night while drunk. Shortly afterwards, a boatload of men crossing the river heard the man's feeble cries for help and managed to locate him in the darkness. 'When taken up no signs of life appeared', reported the newspaper, but 'the means recommended [for resuscitation] in such cases being made use of, he was after some time recovered.'[23]

Most people weren't so lucky – hence the setting up of the Humane Society, the first meeting of which was on 7 March 1791.[24] Robert Darwin attended, along with a number of other medical men. He donated a guinea, which enabled him to be a director of the society, and he also sat on its committee. They appointed two 'receiving houses', one at 'The Friars' (presumably St Julian's) and the other at Mardol Quay. These houses were equipped with 'an apparatus' (for resuscitation), and 'drags' (presumably some sort of lifebelt) to enable the drowning person to be pulled from the river. The Humane Society Committee ordered that a request be sent to the Salop Infirmary that the hospital should be open at all times to receive casualties. They also gave financial rewards to people who opened their houses for the receipt of casualties, and to those who raised the alarm or assisted in the rescue.[25] The reward given 'to every medical gentleman by whose means a person apparently dead, shall be recovered' was a silver medal. (Medals are still awarded by the Royal Humane Society for bravery, especially in relating to victims of drowning accidents.) In addition to all this, instructions for performing resuscitation were to be placed prominently in public places such as inns, shops and even

The Wedgwood Family in 1780, by George Stubbs. From right to left: Josiah I, Sarah (Sally), John, Josiah II, Susannah, Catherine (Kitty), Thomas, Sarah, Mary Ann. (Courtesy of the Wedgwood Museum Trust, Barlaston, Staffordshire)

private houses. The Shrewsbury branch of the Humane Society lasted for over fifty years, until it was wound up in 1848 due to lack of funds.[26]

By 1796, after ten years in practice, Robert Darwin was well on the way to financial security, so he felt that at the age of thirty it was time to proceed with marriage. Robert's choice of bride was Susannah Wedgwood, the eldest child of his father's great friend Josiah. Like Erasmus Darwin, Josiah Wedgwood was a man of extraordinary ability. Trained as an ordinary potter, he applied the developing study of chemistry to the production of new and exciting glazes for his china through a painstaking process of experimentation. This scientific work was encouraged by his friendship with Erasmus Darwin and other members of the Lunar Society. He was also an excellent businessman, and built the national and international reputation of the Wedgwood firm within a generation. Josiah was a man of immense courage, as evidenced by the fact that he had to have a leg amputated without anaesthetic, and afterwards learned to walk with an artificial limb.

The prospect of Robert and Susannah's wedding delighted both fathers, formalising the friendship between them that went back over thirty years. Erasmus Darwin had known Josiah Wedgwood's children since they had been very young, and he had a high regard for Susannah. He wrote to Robert that, 'I am happy to hear you are so near the time of your marriage with a lady whom I have always esteemed, as an accomplished lady, with a distinct understanding and an excellent heart ... '[27]

Susannah had been born in January 1765, much loved and cherished from her birth. Her mother, Sally, expressed this love when she wrote to her brother-in-law that her new baby 'was worth travelling 150 miles to see'![28] Susannah wasn't an only child for long. John arrived next in 1766, with Richard the following year. Richard died in his first year, so there was a gap of three years between John and the next brother, Josiah II, universally known as Jos. The last brother Thomas (Tom) was born in 1771, and three sisters, Catherine (Kitty), born in 1774, Sarah (1776), and Mary Ann (1778) completed the family.

During Susannah's childhood her father's pottery business grew rapidly, and the family's increased wealth and status was reflected in Josiah being able to build a grand house, Etruria Hall, next to his pottery on the outskirts of Stoke-on-Trent. Josiah gave careful thought to the education of his children. Contrary to much of the received wisdom of the time, Josiah felt that education was just as important for his daughters as for the boys. He had the choice of sending his children away or educating them at home. In the event, he did a bit of both.

Susannah was initially sent to a boarding school in Liverpool, but she did not thrive there, so Josiah decided that her education should continue at home with the rest of the children.[29] Josiah could afford to employ good teachers, and believed that education should consist of far more than just the classics. So in addition they learned French from a native Frenchman recommended by Erasmus Darwin; accounts, with a view to helping later with the business; writing; and chemistry, which Josiah taught himself. They also had art tuition from such luminaries as George Stubbs, most famous for his horse pictures, and Joseph Wright of Derby, another friend of Erasmus Darwin. As well as joining the boys' lessons, the girls also had their own governesses. Amongst these was Everina Wollstonecraft, the younger sister of Mary Wollstonecraft (1759-1797), who would later become famous (or infamous) as the author of perhaps the seminal work on women's rights, *A Vindication of the Rights of Women*. Everina apparently shared these views, so presumably something of this counter-cultural thought rubbed off on the Wedgwood girls.[30]

As a boy Robert Darwin would often travel from his family home in Lichfield to the Wedgwoods at Etruria to join in their lessons. These visits to the relaxed Wedgwood household must have been a welcome respite from the complexities of his own family situation. When he was aged twelve he wrote to Josiah, 'I think every day of the happyness [sic] I enjoyed at Etruria.'[31] Perhaps even then part of his 'happyness' was the chance to spend time with Susannah. He also became a firm friend of each of the Wedgwood boys – their lives would later cross at many points.

Susannah flourished under this educational regime. She became an excellent spinet player, and when the piano became all the rage she even tried to teach Erasmus Darwin to play it, though without success, since he was tone deaf like his grandson Charles! She learned household management from her formidably organised mother Sally, and a love of plants and gardening from both her parents. She became fluent in French, and was later to act as her father's French 'secretary', dealing with the many contacts the Wedgwood company had in France. She also developed an interest in science from her father, whose experiments took place in the basement of Etruria.

To complete her education, Josiah arranged for her to attend Blacklands, a school in Chelsea. While she lived in London she stayed with Thomas Bentley (1731-80), Josiah's greatest friend and business partner, and Bentley's new wife. The Bentleys had no children, so Susannah became like an adopted daughter. During this time she was introduced to London social life, and also developed her Unitarian faith, as the Bentleys were staunch Unitarians like the Wedgwoods. Unitarians sought to interpret the Bible as their reason led them, freed from the doctrines and creeds of the established churches.[32] As the century developed, its defining

Susannah Wedgwood aged fifteen, detail from Wedgwood family portrait. (Courtesy of the Wedgwood Museum Trust, Barlaston, Staffordshire)

feature became more clearly a rejection of the divinity of Christ and the Holy Spirit. They tended to reject 'old-time theories that man was born in sin'[33], and hence traditional views of the necessity of individual salvation through the death of Christ. For this reason, they mostly had an optimistic view of the essential goodness of man and the possibility of his moral and ethical progress. Erasmus Darwin took delight in pouring scorn on Unitarians, including his friend Josiah Wedgwood. Erasmus decried Unitarianism as 'a feather-bed to catch a falling Christian'.[34] He presumably meant that Unitarianism was a refuge for those who were in the process of losing their faith, but couldn't quite go the whole way and become unbelievers.

Susannah must have been deeply saddened, as was her father, by Bentley's sudden and early death, which occurred when she was fifteen. Soon after she returned to Etruria from London her father arranged to have a family portrait painted by Stubbs. Josiah found the whole process tedious in the extreme, and perhaps the rather bored look on his face reflects his actual feelings! He was also dissatisfied with the likenesses of his wife, Mary Ann, and especially Susannah, but even so our eye is drawn to Susannah in the centre of the picture, sitting confidently upright on her beautiful horse. She is dressed in the latest eye-catching fashion – clearly already a young woman of substance in her own right.

After Bentley's death Susannah moved into an independent adult life, and when away from home she frequently corresponded with her father. She wrote of visits to Derby, where Erasmus Darwin and his new family now lived, and where she sometimes attended the Philosophical Society that Darwin had founded. She also often stayed in London, from where she reported to her father that, now that the country was at war with France, he was being criticised for having supported the French Revolution in earlier years. These murmurings of discontent did not

Waterlily design for Susannah's wedding.

develop into physical attacks on Josiah, as had happened in Birmingham to some of the other Lunar Society members, but he knew that he needed to be careful about what he said in future. Susannah also shared his liberal views on social issues such as the abolition of the slave trade, a conviction that she and Robert passed on to their children.

In many ways Robert and Susannah fitted easily together: childhood friends, intellectual equals who moved comfortably in the upper strata of society, both liberal-minded – they had so much in common. The only immediate cloud on the horizon was Josiah's failing health, which resulted in his death on 2 January 1795, Susannah's thirtieth birthday. She felt his loss acutely – she was always her father's favourite, and she loved him dearly in return. She must have been particularly moved that, despite his illness, her father commissioned a special Wedgwood dinner service with a waterlily design as a wedding present.

3

A PERSON OF EMINENCE

Robert and Susannah were married in London in April 1796, when Robert was almost thirty and Susannah was thirty-one. Moving to Shrewsbury must have been both an excitement and a challenge for Susannah. She missed the familiarity of Etruria Hall, with its beautiful gardens that she so much enjoyed. In some ways a town house in Shrewsbury could have seemed a poor exchange, but Shrewsbury had much to offer a well-educated young woman accustomed to moving in 'polite' society. Shortly after this time William Cobbett wrote of the town:

> Shrewsbury is one of the most interesting spots that man ever beheld … It is curiously enclosed by the River Severn, which is here large and fine, and which, in the form of a horseshoe, completely surrounds it … The environs of this town, especially on the Welsh side, are the most beautiful that can be conceived. The town lies in the midst of a fine agricultural country, of which it is the great and almost only mart. Hither come the farmers to sell their produce and hence they take in exchange their groceries, their clothing, and all the materials for their implements and the domestic conveniences … I cannot quit Shrewsbury without expressing the great satisfaction that I derived from my visit to that place.[1]

Shrewsbury was a bustling market town with a population of around 14,500. Its central streets still followed the medieval layout, but the town had developed a great deal over the previous half-century. Boosted by its position on the River Severn, and also by the enormous improvement in the roads, Shrewsbury was a centre for the export of wool and manufactured products and the import of raw materials and fancy goods. The express coaches arrived in London by 9 p.m. the same day, having left Shrewsbury at 5 a.m., so the town had ready access to the capital, and was no longer just an outpost on the Welsh border. Elegant houses were built as county landowners felt the need to have a town base in addition to their country seats. Coffeehouses sprang up, and there was a regular 'season' of social events, culminating in the hunt ball. As we have seen, there was also a vibrant intellectual life, in which Robert Darwin played a part. No doubt he took pleasure in introducing Susannah to his friends and acquaintances, and she would have invited them to their fashionable house in The Crescent, just up the road from Robert's former house in St John's Hill.

The Crescent. (Author's collection)

Robert and Susannah, though, had plans for something much grander than The Crescent. They wanted more room, and a large garden that they could both enjoy. Robert also wanted to make a statement about himself. A correspondent writing to her friend summed it up:

> When Dr Darwin's father enquired why he built so large a house, [Dr Darwin] said, 'Had I built a small one nobody would have enquired about me and would not have supposed a person of eminence could live in such a one – but now I intend my house and name shall introduce me and pay for itself.' And wonderfully has his plan succeeded![2]

So how were they to fund such an ambitious project? Robert was already highly successful in his profession, but a fee income of £2–3,000 a year would not be enough to enable him to build and maintain the projected house. He was gaining income from his investments, and his father had also given him £1,000 when he got married[3] as well as a farm in Lincolnshire, which would provide valuable rental income.[4] But the major change in their finances was the money that Susannah had from her father's will and marriage settlement – the enormous sum of £25,000.[5] All in all, there was plenty to build a house suitable for 'a person of eminence'.

Their plans were temporarily interrupted by a new arrival – Marianne was born at The Crescent on 7 April 1798. The most likely origin of her name is as a variant of 'Mary Ann', after Susannah's disabled youngest sister of that name, who had died twelve years before. Despite having numerous offspring, she was the sixty-six-year-old Erasmus Darwin's first grandchild. Naturally, he was delighted, writing to Robert:

> We are all excessively happy in hearing that Mrs RW Darwin is safe in her bed, and congratulate you both on this addition to your family. I shall now begin to think myself beginning to grow old, having acquired the name of grandfather ... [6]

Even with Marianne's arrival, the planning for the new house went ahead steadily. Robert was keen to find an 'eminent' position to build. The geography of Shrewsbury is such that the old town is huddled together in the loop of the River Severn. At that time there was no room left inside the loop to build the sort of house they envisaged. Looking beyond the old town, they were drawn to an area above the suburb of Frankwell, just west of the town, and joined to it by the Welsh Bridge, which had recently been rebuilt. Above Frankwell, the Holyhead Road climbs steeply as it begins its journey to North Wales. The incline, and the area around it, is called The Mount. On the left of the hill was (and still is) Millington's Hospital, built in 1748-49 to provide education for poor children and accommodation for the elderly.[7] The area at the top of the hill, between the road and the steep drop to another bend in the river, was not then developed. This is where Robert and Susannah chose to build their house. The whole plot amounted to over seven acres (seven acres, three rods and eight perches, to be precise).[8] Situated on the top of the hill, it had stunning views of the old town to the east. Before the trees grew up, there were also pleasant views of the river to the north, from where the house could clearly be seen. It was also originally visible from the road, but a combination of large trees and the lowering of the road to reduce the gradient, which was engineered by Thomas Telford in 1836, means that it is now hidden from that direction. The other benefit of the position was that, being situated on the western side of the town, the prevailing winds blew away the smoke and smells from the tanneries and workshops in Frankwell, and Hazledine's foundry and Burr's lead works in Coleham.

Having decided on the location, what would they call the new house? They chose the name 'The Mount House', a statement that this was the most important house in the area. This feeling of importance is reflected in the fact that it later became known as simply 'The Mount', which is what I shall call it from now on. (The authorities seem to have been confused about what to call it, too. In the 1851 census it was called '53 Frankwell', and in the 1861 census '130 The Mount'!)

The next question to be decided was who would be chosen to design and build the new house. At that time, only the super-rich had their own architects. People such as the Darwins employed an experienced and competent local builder who worked from pattern books inspired by famous architects such as Inigo Jones and John Nash.[9] We do not know exactly who designed and built their house, but the most likely candidate is John Hiram Haycock (1759-1830). For over a century, four generations of the Haycock family were builders and later architects in and around Shrewsbury. John Hiram was responsible for a number of major works, such as the old Shirehall in the Square (1785), the prison (1787-93) and Allatt's School in Murivance (1799).[10] John Hiram's son, William (1791-1870), was even better known, with a vast output of work such as the new Salop Infirmary (1827-30), St George's Church Frankwell (1831-32) and the Music Hall (1839-40). The Haycocks were great friends of the Darwins, as evidenced by the number of times their name is mentioned in Robert Darwin's account books. The Haycocks are also mentioned in the family's correspondence with Charles on HMS *Beagle*.[11]

The Mount, *c.* 1860. (Shrewsbury Museums Service)

The exact date of the building of The Mount is not clear. The Salop Fire Office Policy Book has an entry for 21 October 1797 that 'Robert Waring Darwin MD desires to insure on his new built house of Frankwell near Shrewsbury, brick and slated, not exceeding £900.'[12] The entry then quotes an annual premium of 18s, with a one-off charge for setting up the policy of 6s, making a total of £1 4s. On the face of it, this is clear evidence that the house had been built by October 1797. However, other documentary sources state that Marianne was born at the Crescent in April 1798, while Caroline was born at The Mount in September 1800,[13] which suggests that the family moved at some time between those two dates, even though the house may have been ready earlier.

Robert Darwin's account book provides the best evidence that it was probably John Hiram Haycock who designed and built The Mount, and that the date of completion was 1799. The book records that 'Mr Haycock' was paid £400 on 17.4.1798, and a further £200 on 23.5.1799.[14] Between these entries are a number of quite large payments to other individuals. The entries thus suggest that Haycock's payment was two-thirds of his fee at the beginning of the work, and the final third on completion, the payments to others being for those who actually did the building work. How then can we reconcile this date with The Salop Fire Office Policy Book entry? The answer may be that this was just an estimate, for the rest of the page is blank, except for the word 'dropt' below the entry. The book provides one page per customer, with notes of subscriptions paid, claims and so on over a number of years. Most of the pages have multiple entries, but there is nothing more about The Mount, so I imagine what happened is that Robert asked for a preliminary estimate before the house was built, but he did not take it up, perhaps due to delay in building the house.

The Mount, which is now used as offices, is a typical late Georgian house facing south. It has five bays and there is little in the way of external ornamentation, save for a string-course between the ground and first floors. There is also a solid-looking porch supported by unornamented columns. The house was originally symmetrical, apart from a conservatory at its eastern end. This conservatory was replaced by a larger version in 1834, which in turn was replaced by a brick extension, probably in the early twentieth century.[15] On the ground floor the principal rooms were a dining room, drawing room, morning room (which opened into the conservatory) and library. Upstairs there were fourteen bedrooms, some with dressing rooms. There was also a butler's chamber, coachman's room, valet's room, servants' hall, housekeeper's room, housemaid's closet, butler's pantry, scullery, larder, boot room and cellar. Outside there were extensive outbuildings, grouped around a well in the yard. These were a coal store, brew house, dairy, laundry, coach house and sheds, with two stables, piggery and poultry house. All in all, not a bad establishment for a physician in a market town!

As various institutional owners have extensively altered the house in the last eighty years or so, it is very difficult now to see how the inside of the house would have looked in the days of the Darwins. We can still imagine, though, how Dr Darwin used it for seeing his patients, who, rich and poor alike, entered by the front door. Here they immediately turned left and waited in a small room whose entrance is beneath the elegant cantilevered staircase. From this room they were called into the doctor's consulting room, which in turn led via the dining room to the private part of the house. In this way the doctor did not have to run the gauntlet of the patients in the waiting room when he went to his consulting room.

The furnishings probably reflected the slightly austere look of the house itself, as well as Robert's character – a mixture of generosity and frugality.[16] The drawing room cost £400 to furnish and decorate, and Robert treated Susannah to an organ costing £200, which for some reason resided in the dining room. They spent £59 14s on their own bed and curtains, £47 6s on the bed and its curtains for the next best room, £14 8s on the bed in the housekeeper's room, and £15 5s on a bed for a manservant. Robert and Susannah's bedroom was decorated in blue.

There was a special chair for the doctor, and weighing scales for the consulting room that cost ten guineas. Gradually they built up an impressive library of books with hundreds of volumes, some rare and valuable. In the stables outside there was a chaise costing £145 12s, and a phaeton that was bought for £91; probably Robert usually used the former and Susannah the latter. A fishing stool, which presumably Charles would later use, cost 6s 6d, and all the bells and springs which the family used to summon the servants cost seven guineas.[17]

Such an establishment needed plenty of servants. The censuses of 1841, 1851 and 1861 indicate that there were about seven servants who lived in, the nature of their duties varying according to the needs of the house.[18] The butler and housekeeper were the most important servants. For many years these were Edward Evans and his wife.[19] Edward was obviously well rewarded, for on his death in 1846 he left an estate worth £500 (around £20,000 by today's prices).[20] After he died the Darwins only employed a housekeeper, who in the censuses of 1851 and 1861 was Jane Grice, an unmarried woman who was born in Rodington, between Shrewsbury and Wellington. There was also a ladies' maid, one or two housemaids, a kitchen maid and while Robert Darwin was alive there was a manservant. In 1841 this was Thomas Thurger, who was with his master when he died. A coachman assisted the manservant when he wasn't needed to drive the coaches or look after the horses. For many years the coachman was Mark Briggs, who lived with his family just down the road at 47 Frankwell (later renumbered 125 The Mount). The Darwins also employed a gardener, who in later times lived next door to the coachman at 46 Frankwell. In the 1840s and 1850s the gardener was John Abberley, who certainly knew his plants, though he found writing more challenging, judging by a letter he sent to Charles Darwin after the latter had requested botanical information.[21] Finally, there was a labourer or groom, presumably a man who helped out with the heavy work in the house or garden.

Susannah was an excellent household manager, a talent learned from her mother. The Mount was immaculately kept, the servants smartly dressed in their uniforms. There was much beautiful Wedgwood pottery on display, for which Susannah insisted on paying.[22] She organised two 'great feasts' each year for the other doctors and medical officials in the area, to which the members of the nobility were also invited.[23]

Once they had moved in, Robert and Susannah set about designing the garden, for both had inherited the love of gardening that their fathers shared. It fell to Susannah, however, to do most of the practical organising, as Robert was continually busy with his medical work. She did not just enjoy looking at flowers, but was very much a practical gardener, who would

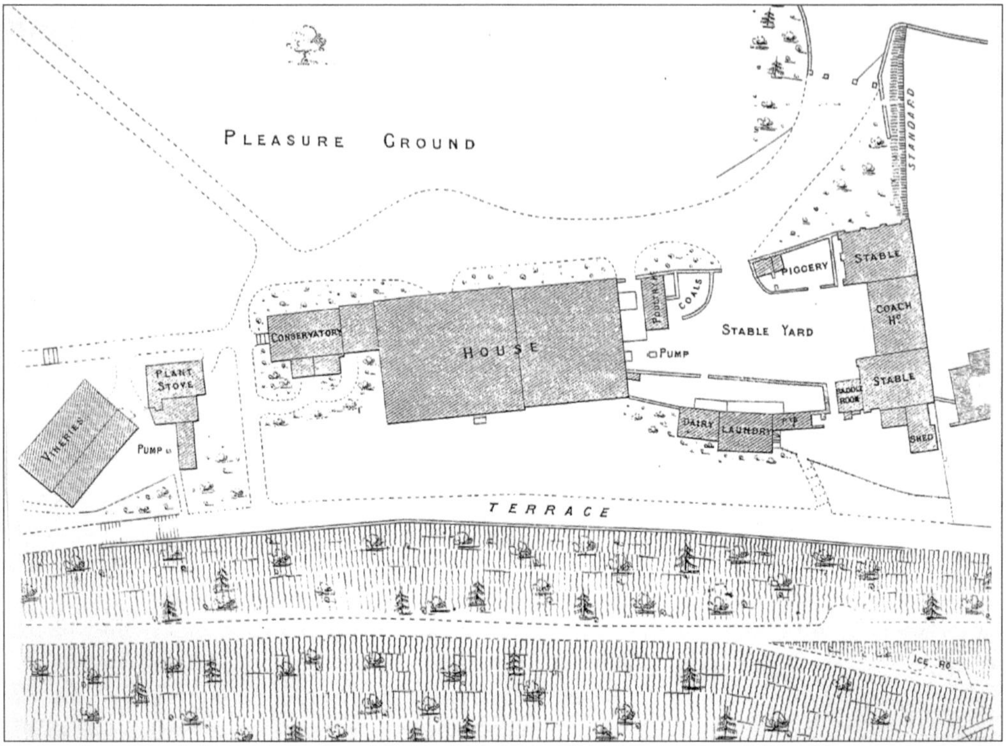

Plan of The Mount grounds, 1866. (Shrewsbury Museums Service)

later pass on her love of plants to her son Charles. Many years later a young school friend of Charles remembered 'his bringing a flower to school and saying that his mother had taught him how by looking at the inside of the blossom the name of the plant could be discovered'.[24] Susannah often corresponded with her brothers John and Jos on the subject of gardening. John was an outstanding botanist – he helped to form the Royal Horticultural Society in 1804, and was its first secretary.

In front of the house was an extensive lawn, in the centre of which was a cedar tree that is still standing. In the lawn Susannah planted a large number of crocuses, which made a magnificent display in the spring.[25] More trees were planted near the road to screen the house from the prevailing winds, and a network of paths was laid out enclosing flower beds, and eventually leading to an enormous kitchen garden in the far corner of the property. Next to the kitchen garden was a circular feature, which drew the walker on to explore the tree-covered terracing that covered the steep slope between the house and the river. There was a path by the river along the full length of the property – at the far end one could scramble back up the terracing to return to the house via the stable yard.[26] As well as being an expert gardener, Susannah was also well known for breeding beautiful doves.[27] Many years later 'their beauty, variety and tameness' were still remembered in the neighbourhood.[28] It is surely not a coincidence that Charles later wrote much on the subject of breeding pigeons, though he did not seem to remember this as one of his mother's loves.

Only a fragment of the garden Susannah created now remains. But in our mind's eye we can imagine the sea of crocuses in the lawn in spring, the immaculate kitchen garden, and the terraced paths dropping down to the river, with the beautiful doves providing a gentle backdrop of sound. Charles was indeed fortunate to grow up in such an environment, which must have helped to stimulate his fascination with nature.

Robert and Susannah's marriage seems to have been genuinely happy. She always wrote of him as 'the doctor', a term of affection and respect. Their marriage settlement was carefully drawn up to ensure Susannah was well provided for.[29] In an early will drawn up in 1808, Susannah (along with her brother Jos) is named as one of Robert's executors – it was fairly unusual for a woman to be named as an executor at that time.[30] The household account books also take care to identify that part of the investment income that was Susannah's (£7,172 14s 6d between 1795-1804, rising to £16,344 5s 5d by 1815).[31] The entries concerning her own money or those relating to the accounts of her brothers Jos and Tom are in a different hand, presumably her own, indicating that she was actively involved in the family finances.

One of the most difficult tasks of any historian is to try to separate fact from bias, half-truths and the assertions of previous generations of writers. This is especially difficult with regard to identifying what a historical person was really like, since people are often complex, and their characters may appear self-contradictory and change over time. Untangling the truth about the characters of Robert and Susannah Darwin is particularly challenging. In some quarters they have had a pretty bad press, especially Robert.[32] These writers tend to portray him as a domestic tyrant, ruling his family with a rod of iron, with Susannah little more than a nobody, subservient to his every whim and fancy, but the truth seems to be far removed from this caricature.

Before her marriage she had the best possible education available in those days, especially for a girl. Many girls could play well on keyboard instruments, but few were also fluent in French, able to keep accounts and have an interest in science and the arts, as well as botany and garden design. She knew her own mind, and was influenced by the early version of women's liberation. Susannah brought this broad range of accomplishments into her marriage. Robert and Susannah's love affair may not have been intensely passionate, but it was obviously a genuine love match between two mature friends. What may appear as inconsequential details show the trust and closeness of their relationship. The organ bought for £200 (four years' wages for a skilled man), the 'his' and 'hers' carriages in the stables, the way she maintained control over her inherited wealth, even the fact that she was an executor of his draft will – all these facts point towards a lady of skill and independence, whose relationship with her husband was that of equality.

Early in their married life Robert and Susannah had to cope with three painful bereavements. The first was the death of Robert's older brother Erasmus, who by this time had become a successful lawyer, so successful that, though he was only just forty, he was considering retiring from the law to live the life of a country gentleman.[33] In mid-November 1799 he had written Susannah a cheerful letter explaining his plans, but there was one cloud on the horizon – his accounts. His ability to keep on top of his book keeping was as poor as Robert's was good. Erasmus had a deadline of the end of the year to finish his accounts, so he worked long and hard on them over Christmas. Then, late at night on 29 December, he was found drowned, having fallen into the river at the end of his garden in Derby. The cause was, of course, unknown. His father, Erasmus senior, was convinced it was an accident, but the circumstances would seem to suggest that suicide was a more likely verdict.

Whatever the cause, Erasmus senior was heartbroken, and this seems to have been the beginning of the end for him, as he died in April 1802, just over two years later. Robert later recalled that 'his father had found it a constant exertion to obtain relief from the thought of his son's death', and Erasmus' biographer concludes that 'although Erasmus lived on for over two years his joie de vivre died on 29th December 1799.'[34] What added to the family's pain was that after his death his long-term friend Anna Seward published a critical biography of Erasmus senior, including the accusation that the relationship between the father and the son had been bad, and Erasmus senior had been relieved at this son's death. This greatly angered Robert, who demanded a retraction. A contentious correspondence ensued, with something of an apology from Anna Seward,[35] but the older man's reputation had been much damaged, from which it would take a very long time to recover.

The third bereavement was that of Susannah's youngest brother, Tom. Tom was the most intelligent of her three brothers, witty and companionable, and a great favourite of all the family. He moved in a literary circle and counted as his friends Samuel Taylor Coleridge, Robert Southey, William Wordsworth and Charles and Mary Lamb, among others. He was also involved in scientific experimentation, collaborating with the young Humphry Davy. One of the subjects he studied was fixing light with silver salts, the basis of photography, but he did not live long enough to make it work in practice.

Tom, however, had an undiagnosed illness, one symptom of which was excruciating headaches. Among the many doctors he consulted was Dr Erasmus Darwin, who started him on large doses of the opiate laudanum. Whether it was for this reason or due to his association with Coleridge, Tom seems to have added opiate addiction to his increasingly debilitating illness. Desperate to help Tom, Robert persuaded one of his colleagues, Dr Thomas DuGard,[36] to take time off from his practice, travel to the south of England and stay with Tom as long as was needed to help him. By being away for a long time Dr DuGard upset not only his own patients, but also some of his colleagues who had to cover for him.[37] DuGard's opinion of the hopelessness of Tom's case was the same as Robert's, but it was a reassurance to Robert and Susannah to know that he agreed that nothing more could be done, and Tom died soon after, on 10 July 1805. For this service Susannah paid Dr DuGard £100.[38]

The newly married couple did not have much time to brood on their losses, however – there was plenty to do with a new Darwin family!

4

THE NEW FAMILY

For the five years or so after the Darwin family had moved into The Mount, much of Susannah's time was taken up with pregnancy or small babies. Caroline Sarah was born in September 1800, Susan Elizabeth in August 1803, and Erasmus Alvey followed on the fifth anniversary of his Uncle Erasmus' death (29 December 1804).[1] Susan was named after her mother, and Erasmus after his uncle and grandfather, but who Caroline was named after is not obvious.

The children having arrived, how were they to be brought up? Robert and Susannah's different views on religion provided one challenge. Susannah became fully involved in the life of the Unitarian Chapel in Shrewsbury's High Street, and was one of the signatories to a letter inviting Revd George Augustus Case to fill the vacancy.[2, 3] Robert Darwin was a religious sceptic like his father, but mostly he kept his views as hidden as he could. Charles illustrated this when he wrote that his father's advice to him before he got engaged to be married was:

> To conceal carefully my doubts, for he said that he had known extreme misery thus caused with married persons. Things went on pretty well until the wife or husband became out of health, and then some women suffered miserably by doubting about the salvation of their husbands, thus making them likewise to suffer.[4]

Like his father Erasmus, Robert was an evolutionist. He demonstrated his belief in evolution by having bookplates printed in 1795 with exactly the same motto that his father had used – 'E Conchis Omnia'.[5] On the other hand, Robert's standing in society, and hence his ability to attract patients, might be compromised by too open a demonstration of such views, so to the onlooker he appeared a respectable, if not devout, Anglican. He was also well aware that Unitarianism was still technically illegal (it did not become legal until 1813), so he kept clear of his wife's religion.

This conflict between Robert and Susannah's views on religion can be discerned in their decisions regarding the baptism of the children.[6] Marianne was baptised at the High Street Chapel on 30 April 1798, but was also christened at St Chad's Anglican Church the following day. The underlying message from this seems to be Susannah saying to Robert, 'I am going to ensure that my girls are brought up to follow my faith, but I don't mind them also being christened in the Anglican Church for the sake of your reputation.' When Erasmus senior wrote

Susannah Darwin in 1793, by Peter Paillou. (Dr Milo Keynes)

to Robert shortly after, he referred to Marianne as 'the little Presbyterian'[7], which suggests that he realised that the little girl was to be brought up as a nonconformist. (The High Street Chapel was still officially Presbyterian, to avoid conflicting with the law that Unitarianism was illegal.) The same baptism arrangements occurred with the next two girls, though in these cases the christening at St Chad's preceded baptism at the chapel. Caroline was christened at St Chad's on 14 September 1800, and baptised at the chapel on 12 October 1800; Susan was christened at St Chad's on 3 August 1803, and baptised in the chapel on 17 August 1803.

If Susannah had her way with the girls' religious upbringing, the boys were in Robert's jurisdiction. We can see this by the fact that neither Erasmus nor Charles was baptised at the High Street Chapel. They were christened at St Chad's, but in both cases the event occurred over nine months after the boys were born (on 26 September 1805 for Erasmus, and 15 November 1809 for Charles). It seems as if Susannah was saying to Robert, 'I accept that you won't have the boys baptised as nonconformists, but if you want them christened at St Chad's you will have to organise it yourself.' The inordinate time delay probably reflected the low priority Robert gave to the ceremony. When Catherine[8] was born in 1810, it was 'business as usual', with a baptism at the chapel and a christening at St Chad's taking place the same day. These religious differences were reflected throughout the children's lives. Marianne's religious views are not recorded, but the other three girls all continued as committed Unitarians.[9] On the other hand, the boys both lived their later lives as unbelievers.

Four pregnancies in six years took a heavy toll on Susannah's health. For a number of years before this time she had had various ailments, including a bad bout of rheumatic fever about the time of her marriage, which could have left her with a weak heart.[10, 11] If this was so, it may

Robert Darwin's bookplate. (Shropshire Archives)

have been the reason for her second pregnancy (with Caroline) being described as difficult,[12] and for her needing several months' bed rest while carrying Susan.[13] After this time she was frequently ill with headaches, intestinal upsets and general malaise, being described as 'never quite well, and never quite ill.'[14] These difficult pregnancies seem to have aged her, for she more than once remarked that, 'everyone seems young but me'.[15] With Susannah effectively out of action for months at a time, and Robert always busy, this must have been a very difficult time for the family. These difficulties were probably the reason for the two oldest girls being described by an aunt as 'children who are more rude and disagreeable than any I ever knew'.[16] The young Darwins even appear to have had their mother 'in subjection', as Susannah's sister-in-law recorded.[17]

Susannah's low state could have been partly brought on by post-natal depression, which was, of course, unrecognised as such in those days. Susannah had plenty of reasons to suffer from it, which included the loss of independence that relatively late motherhood brings, multiple bereavements and difficult pregnancies. So, despite having plenty of practical help about the house, in her low physical and mental state she could not prevent the strong-willed young children getting the better of her.

She may not have been helped in disciplining the children by the Darwin and Wedgwood approach to child rearing. In this they were 'progressives', following the likes of the French philosopher Rousseau (1712-78).[18] Traditional child rearing at that time was based on the Biblical concept that every child is born with 'original sin', that is a tendency to do wrong when faced with choices in life. So an important part of traditional child rearing, and also formal education, was to mould the child's stubborn and unruly will by corporal punishment if that was necessary. In contrast to this approach, 'Rousseau's theory of education rests on two assumptions: that man

St Chad's Church, *c.* 1850. (Henry Pidgeon, *Memorials of Shrewsbury* J.H. Leake, Shrewsbury, 1850)

is by nature good, and that society and civilisation corrupt the native goodness.'[19] Child rearing according to these principles should thus allow children to express themselves as much as possible, and discipline should be minimal, or even non-existent. Whatever one believes about human nature, it is generally agreed that children need boundaries. A new inexperienced mother finds this difficult enough; if she is depressed it may be almost impossible.

And where was Robert while all this was going on? Probably he left looking after small children to his wife and the servants. He was always busy with his medical work, part of which was looking after other people's children. His own early experiences, with various mother substitutes and a father who was often distracted and overbearing, had not given him an obvious role model to follow as he learned to be a father. Robert, too, suffered from depression on and off throughout his life. At these times he became moody, irritable, angry (especially with outsiders, such as Anna Seward) and authoritarian with the family. Much later, his son Charles wrote of his father, that 'he was generally in high spirits and laughed and joked with everyone – often with his servants – with the utmost freedom, yet he had the art of making everyone obey him to the letter.'[20]

Unitarian Church plaque in memory of Charles Darwin. (Author's collection)

But by the time that Charles was born that February day in 1809, the family seems to have become much more harmonious. Susannah had had a break of over four years between pregnancies, the children were growing up and the period of family bereavements was over. In many ways Charles had a very favoured upbringing. The family was rich and their home very luxurious by the standards of the day. As a young boy he enjoyed playing in the extensive gardens, often with Catherine, who was close to him in age. When he was older he fished in the river at the bottom of the garden, and enjoyed other solitary pleasures. He was an unremarkable, self-sufficient sort of child, content with reading, going on walks by himself or following the servants round as they went about their duties. He adored Marianne, Caroline and Susan ('the sisterhood', as he called them[21]). They all, in turn, doted on him. Perhaps because of their mother's frequent illnesses, Caroline in particular was charged with the care of Charles and Catherine, and Charles' earliest memory is of sitting on Caroline's knee while she cut an orange up for him.[22] Fond as he was of his sisters, he was particularly close to his brother Erasmus.

Because Charles could later remember so little about his mother, it is hard to know how close their relationship was. She was frequently ill, but was able to organise the house and garden and share her love of plants with Charles. Susannah also took Charles with the rest of the children to the Unitarian Chapel, as recorded by a plaque on the wall of the sanctuary, though the words that Charles 'was a constant worshipper' there seem a little far-fetched. The family often visited the Wedgwoods at Maer in Staffordshire, and sometimes the wider family would go away together, as when they all rented a house in Bath for a fortnight in 1815.[23] Doubtless, Susannah related to Charles during these and many other times, but her influence was too early in his life to be remembered in detail by him.

His relationship with his father Robert, though, would be one of the key factors in his life. Far from being 'a repressive and awesome influence – a figure inculcating fear and restraint,' as one writer has stated,[24] Robert seems to have been a generally positive and benign influence on the young Charles. Much later, Caroline remembered the rapport between father and son. She wrote:

> Instead of being 'a naughty boy' [Charles] was particularly affectionate, tractable and sweet tempered, and my father had the highest opinion of his understanding and intelligence. My father was very fond of him, and even when he was a little boy of 6 or 7, however bustled and overtired, often had Charles with him when dressing to teach him some little thing such as the Almanack – and Charles used to be so eager to be down in time. Charles does not seem to have known half how much my father loved him.[25]

Robert also gave Charles his first books on geology and natural history, items of great sentimental value to Robert, since they were the only remaining possessions of his oldest brother, Charles' namesake.[26]

When he just turned eight, in the spring of 1817, Charles began to attend a small day school run by Revd George Case, the Unitarian minister. This was at 13 Claremont Hill in the centre of Shrewsbury, and its rear windows overlooked the churchyard of the new St Chad's Church. Charles walked each day the mile or so from The Mount through Frankwell, across the Welsh Bridge and along Barker Street, trying to avoid the stray dogs that roamed round the area. Presumably, this school was Susannah's choice, though Robert was probably happy, since Mr Case was known as an erudite man, not given to religious controversy. Charles' rather sheltered upbringing made him feel like 'a simple little fellow'[27] as he related with the older boys, but his open nature encouraged friendships, some of which lasted into adult life. He was deeply moved when the school watched from their back windows as William Matthews, dragoon soldier from the 15th Hussars, was buried with full military honours in St Chad's churchyard.[28, 29] This took place on 23 August 1817, and no doubt reminded Charles of the recent tragedy in his young life.

Just a few months before, Susannah's ill health suddenly became acute. She developed severe abdominal pains, most likely from peritonitis (which is due to leakage of stomach or intestinal contents into the abdominal cavity). Her sister Kitty rushed over from Maer, but could see there was little hope of recovery. Kitty wrote to the rest of her family:

> The Dr [Robert Darwin] has not the slightest hope … The pain indeed is gone that was her first illness, but she has such severe vomitings, and sickness that he says he does not think her sufferings much lessened. She was today for a few hours easier, and the Dr could not help feeling some little doubt whether it was not possible she might recover. This evening she is worse, and he is very wretched. Still though so exceedingly feeble, she has such a tenaciousness of life, that he fears she may suffer for some time … Her senses are as perfect as ever. From feebleness she can hardly speak. She has not seen any of the children but Marianne and Caroline since Friday.[30]

Claremont Hill, *c.* 1905. (Thomas Auden, *Shrewsbury: A Historical and Topographical Account of the Town* Methuen, 1923)

In the event she struggled on for another twenty-four hours or so, eventually dying on Tuesday evening, 15 July 1817. She was buried at St Chad's Church, Montford, which is a village about four miles west of Shrewsbury. Quite why she was not buried at the parish church, St Chad's in Shrewsbury, is a mystery. The esteem in which she was held in the town can be gauged from the fact that a contemporary who kept a diary of significant events in the town noted her death. Normally, he only recorded the deaths of men he considered significant – Susannah is the only lady he considered important enough to be remembered.[31]

The remaining members of the Darwin family coped with their grief in different ways. Robert was utterly devastated. No doubt he was frustrated and angry that his medical knowledge was useless to help his wife, whose death must have been especially painful, as it would have brought back memories of his mother's early death. Like many men, and especially the Darwins, he found it difficult to express his sadness, which worsened his periods of depression, anger and autocratic behaviour. He would never want to marry again, such was his commitment to the only woman he had ever loved.

Marianne (then nineteen) and Caroline (nearly seventeen) did at least have the satisfaction of having done what they could for their mother in her last few days. For the younger children, especially Charles and Catherine, it must have been most difficult, since they were too young to really understand, and had not been allowed to see their mother during her final illness, as was the custom in those days. Charles reacted to it all by suppressing every memory of her, 'except her death-bed, her black velvet gown, and her curiously constructed work-table'.[32] He stated that 'my forgetfulness is partly due to my sisters, owing to their great grief, never being able to speak about her or mention her name,'[33] but that seems not to be strictly true.[34] Be that as it may, her death certainly had a profound effect on all the members of the Darwin household.

Rear of Revd Case's school from St Chad's churchyard. (Author's collection)

5

'SIMPLY A BLANK'

After Susannah's death, life slowly took on a new pattern for the Darwin family. Robert coped with his grief by throwing himself even more into his work. Marianne organised the household, while Susan was more involved with helping her father. One of Caroline's roles was the supervision of Charles and Catherine. Erasmus was already a boarder at Shrewsbury School. The household has been described as a 'teenage matriarchy'[1], but the experience of bereavement seems to have encouraged a bond of genuine affection between the siblings, rather than the dictatorship that the expression suggests. For example, Charles wrote at about this time that, 'I like Mariane [sic] excessively, she is so very good to Miss Jones [probably a housemaid]'.[2]

Caroline was sixteen when her mother died, and she seems to have been a particular favourite with her father. Her aunt wrote of her, 'Doctor Darwin is always very kind and very fond of Caroline … '[3] She was also a favourite with her uncle Jos (Josiah Wedgwood II). Her strong personality and sense of humour reminded him of his sister Susannah, Caroline's mother.[4]

Caroline's role as Charles' and Catherine's teacher had been present for some time, and she now became the nearest thing to a surrogate mother to them. She remembered those times with great affection, writing to Charles later:

> It made me feel quite melancholy the other day looking at your old garden and the flowers just coming up which you used to be so happy watching. I think the time when you and Catherine were little children and I was always with you or thinking about you was the happiest part of my life, and I dare say will always be.[5]

Charles' view of her was a bit different. He wrote that:

> Caroline was extremely kind, clever and zealous; but she was too zealous in trying to improve me. For I clearly remember after this long interval of years, saying to myself when about to enter a room where she was – 'what will she blame me for now?' and I made myself dogged so as not to care what she might say.[6]

Shrewsbury School as it looked in Charles Darwin's day, artist unknown. (Shrewsbury Museums Service)

Charles seems to have had little insight into the fact that it was hardly surprising that his sister might become authoritarian, given that at the age of sixteen she had suddenly been thrust into a role for which she was unprepared, while struggling to come to terms with losing her mother.

For the time being, Charles continued to attend Mr Case's school, but the plan had always been that he would join Erasmus at Shrewsbury School, and this duly happened about a year after their mother's death. Charles was then nine years old, and Erasmus was thirteen. The brothers were different in many ways, but remained close throughout their lives. Charles' summary of his brother's character was that:

> My brother Erasmus possessed a remarkably clear mind, with extensive and diversified tastes and knowledge in literature, art, and even in science … He was extremely agreeable, and his wit often reminded me of that in the letters and works of Charles Lamb. He was very kind-hearted; but his health from his boyhood had been weak, and as a consequence he failed in energy. His spirits were not high, sometimes low, more especially during early and middle manhood. He read much, even whilst a boy, and at school encouraged me to read, lending me books.[7]

Shrewsbury School's correct name was the Royal Free Grammar School. It was then housed in what is now the Shrewsbury Borough Library in Castle Gates. It was 'royal' because it was established by a charter of King Edward VI in 1551. It was 'free' because it was outside the jurisdiction of the Bishop of Lichfield and Coventry. (It was also 'free' in that the income from its endowments made it possible for sons of Shrewsbury burgesses to attend free of charge.) Finally, it was 'grammar' because its primary purpose was the teaching of the ancient languages, Latin and Greek, rather than practical subjects. Soon after its foundation it became a 'public'

Revd Samuel Butler, by Thomas Kirby. (Courtesy of Shrewsbury School)

school, that is open to boarders from anywhere in the country. So Erasmus and Charles, even though they lived barely a mile from the school, became boarders, paying £42 a year each for boarding, and 8 guineas for tuition.[8]

The emotional effect on Charles of this transition to boarding school at such a young age and so soon after the death of his mother has been debated by historians. For example, one writer considers that, for Charles, school was an escape from the 'teenage matriarchy', and the uncertain temper of his father.[9] Charles wrote later that boarding allowed him 'the great advantage of living the life of a true school-boy,[10] and he was able to enjoy some home comforts once he learned that he could run home for a short while in the evenings without being missed. Having Erasmus, who was kind and protective towards his younger brother, must have also helped Charles to make the transition to the big school.

The other view, which the author tends towards, is that going away to board at Shrewsbury School was an even bigger emotional shock for Charles than the loss of his mother, and that the two events in such quick succession had a profound effect on him for the rest of his life.[11] For, although Shrewsbury School was designed to cater for the sons of the gentry, it was far from genteel. In the distant past the school had had a great reputation, but by 1798 things had deteriorated so badly that discipline had collapsed, and there were only about twenty boys left in the school, only two of whom were fee-paying. The Masters of St John's College, Cambridge, who were responsible for the appointment of the schoolteachers, therefore sacked all the staff, and appointed one of their number, Revd Samuel Butler, as the new headmaster. Butler was then just twenty-four-years-old, with little experience as a schoolmaster, but during his thirty-eight years as headmaster the school was revolutionised. He faced many battles – establishing discipline among the boys, complaints from the town council and long-term friction with his deputy, John Jeudwine, being some of the major issues. Fortunately, by 1818, when Charles started, the school had already gained an enviable reputation for outstanding classical scholarship, its old boys going on to win many of the highest university accolades. This growing reputation was reflected by a rapid increase in the numbers of boys at the school – in 1817 there were seventy boarders, but by 1818 the number had risen to eighty-one.

But with the growth of the school came an acute pressure on space. Many of the boarders were accommodated in the houses in School Lane, which Butler managed to buy, one by one, as his finances allowed. The one next to the school was nicknamed 'Brommy's' after Mrs Bromfield, the matron. This was where Charles lived, and in the arch above the gate can still be seen the initials 'SB', put there originally by Samuel Butler. In her care for the boys 'Brommy' was supported by Mrs Butler. A plump and motherly woman, many Old Salopians remembered her with 'affectionate gratitude for the many kindnesses she showed them during their schooldays.'[12] Kindness, which the tender-hearted Charles craved, was often in short supply. The beds were damp, and often had to be shared. The food was awful, and needed supplementation with rations sent from home or bought in the town. Washing facilities were minimal, which resulted in Caroline upbraiding Charles for his lack of cleanliness.[13] The memory of the smell of one dormitory still turned Charles' stomach years later.

School life was far from peaceful. Just as Charles started at the school there was what has been described as an 'Epidemic of Turbulence'.[14] This was a particularly severe outbreak of bad behaviour amongst some of the boys, which included 'boar hunting' with a neighbouring farmer's pigs, starting fights in the town, breaking windows in the school library and headmaster's study, and posting a placard in the hall threatening Dr Butler with personal violence. The curious thing was that such outbreaks occurred at the same time in almost all of the public schools in England. In Shrewsbury School there were various grievances aired, chiefly around the food, but perhaps the boys were merely reflecting the mood of society as a whole. The years after the Napoleonic Wars were full of unrest, with high food prices, much unemployment and political discontent. This was the period of the 'Peterloo' massacre, Luddites breaking machines in factories and 'Captain Swing' doing great damage in rural areas. The Government probably wished that it proved as easy to contain these disturbances as the 'turbulence' at Shrewsbury School, which Butler had managed to quash by the end of the year.

Doubtless the nine-year-old Charles was not involved in these disturbances, but he could not have been unaware of the unrest in the school. Despite his father being the school doctor, Charles was not allowed any perks. For example, a letter from his father requesting an extra blanket after he had a bout of scarlet fever was met with a firm rebuff from Butler.[15] In matters of school discipline Butler was strict, though usually fair, but when it came to disputes between boys he tended to let them get on with it. He wrote to a parent in 1820:

> The disputes of boys are best settled among themselves ... when two boys quarrel, though battles ought not to be encouraged, perhaps the most desirable thing is that they should settle it between themselves by a trial of mastery, which generally puts a stop to further squabbles.[16]

'Fagging', where younger boys became the servants (or 'douls') of the older ones, was common. This could result in bullying, with vulnerable younger boys sometimes being birched or punished in other unpleasant ways. Charles mentions nothing of this in his memoirs – either he had forgotten these things after the passage of over half a century, or else he avoided such excesses. Perhaps having an older brother at the school and the other boys knowing that his

The house next to Shrewsbury School, with SB (Samuel Butler) above the gates. (Author's collection)

father was the school doctor helped him to avoid being bullied. Many boys could not tolerate the place, and were either removed by their parents or ran away.

Charles coped with school by becoming even more introspective and dreamy. He and Erasmus developed a circle of friends, which made school less unpleasant, but the best he could say of his school days was that they were a complete waste of time. He wrote, 'Nothing could have been worse for the development of my mind than Dr Butler's school, as it was strictly classical, nothing else being taught except a little geography and history. The school as a means of education to me was simply a blank.'[17] He was not the first in his family to feel that way, for his grandfather Erasmus had stated that 'the vigour of the mind languished in the pursuit of classical elegance.'[18]

Butler was adamant that the school was not for teaching 'reading, writing and accounts', when he defended the school against possible parliamentary incursion in the curriculum.[19] Butler wrote that the school's purpose was 'for teaching the learned languages ONLY' (his capitals). Even maths was not on the regular curriculum, though subjects such as writing and maths were available as extras on the Tuesday half-day. The thought of teaching or learning science made Butler's blood boil, and, catching wind that Charles and Erasmus were indulging in chemistry experiments at home, he publicly rebuked the younger boy, calling him a 'poco curante', Italian for 'one who believes in insignificant things'[20], and as Charles had no idea what the words meant, the incident further increased his sense of alienation. Nothing that Butler or the other masters did was able to stimulate any enthusiasm on Charles' part for the classics.

But at least there were the holidays to look forward to. Charles spent as much time as he could out of doors – taking long solitary walks, fishing, collecting insects and birds' eggs, and, later, shooting. Occasionally he would squeeze into his father's coach and accompany him on visits to patients, observing and commenting on the countryside through which they passed. Thus the varied Shropshire countryside became the perfect breeding ground for his later passion for natural history.

The Darwin family also had a large circle of friends and acquaintances. Visits lasting a week or more were regular occurrences, especially to the Owen family at Woodhouse, near Rednal, off the Shrewsbury to Oswestry road, or to Maer Hall, just over the Staffordshire border, which was the home of Jos and Bessy Wedgwood and their large brood. Charles was most interested in the shooting, while the girls, especially Susan and Catherine, revelled in being free of their responsibilities at home. Susan was the prettiest of the daughters, and, it was said that at one time she and her sister Catherine were 'always running after anything in trousers'.[21]

During the later part of Charles' time at Shrewsbury School, Caroline was putting her teaching abilities to good use. It appears that it was on her initiative that the family started a school for the poor children of Frankwell. This was situated in the grounds of Millington's Hospital, just down the road from the Mount.[22] Her aunt wrote:

> I have been with her [Caroline] today at her infant school. I could scarcely refrain from tears of sorrow, at seeing the little creatures, all at the word of command, drop down on their knees and say the Lord's Prayer. They sung two hymns very tolerably, and a whole set of them, none more than four years old, seemed to me quite perfect in their multiplication table. I was quite surprised at their proficiency; not that they were all quite under command, for some of the newcomers were toddling about the room without knowing what they were about, and others were lying down upon a bed that was placed in a corner of a room for that purpose.

Caroline means to send you down the report, if she can get it ready for Lady Bath, as we think it will show at once the necessary expenses, and all that she may want to know. At the same time the reality is not so picturesque as the description, which a person who wishes to put it into practice must be prepared for. She must not expect to see rosy little cherubs in white frocks and pink sashes, but on the contrary perhaps, for the most part, sickly and dirty little children. But this will enhance the virtue of those who seek them out. I admire Caroline's animation about it, her perseverance, her gentleness to the children, and I thought all the time how happy the man who should call her his wife, and how much I should like my Joe [Josiah Wedgwood III] to be that man.[23]

These words were written in 1824, as the school was being established.[24] Caroline's original school was in premises rented from Millington's Hospital. In 1833, the hospital (of which Robert was an active trustee) allowed the Darwins to build a new school on their land, the cost of £300 being paid for by Robert.[25, 26] Susan and Catherine later joined Caroline in the running of the school. The ethos of the school was based on Pestalozzi principles,[27] which were quite revolutionary for the day. Johann Pestalozzi (1746-1827) was one of the founders of modern educational theory. He taught, amongst other things, that 'children should not be given ready-made answers, but should arrive at answers themselves … The aim is to educate the whole child – intellectual education is only part of a wider plan. [Pestalozzi] looked to balance, or keep in equilibrium, three elements – hands, heart and head.'[28] So, especially considering the poverty of the children, the sisters were concerned for their general health and well-being, not just their intellects. An example of this is recorded in a report in the local newspaper that 'Susan and Catherine Darwin celebrated the anniversary of the school in 1849 by providing nearly 200 children with tea and plum cake, followed by games on the 'Doctor's Field'.[29]

Meanwhile, Charles' more expensive education consisted of little more than rote learning. The question, therefore, needs to be asked, 'If Charles Darwin's school experience was so negative, why was Butler and his school so famous and successful?' Butler's obituary in the influential *Quarterly Review* claimed that by his 'example in remodelling our public education' a stimulus was given 'which is now acting on almost all the public schools in the country.'[30] The first thing Butler had had to do at Shrewsbury was re-establish discipline among the pupils, especially among the sons of Shrewsbury burgesses. Butler wrote:

No idea of punishment has ever occurred to the good people of Shrewsbury, because no regular school has been established here for twenty years, so that whenever a boy went home with a report, however true or false, that either himself or any of his schoolfellows had been punished, it furnished matter for observations and ill-natured remarks.[31]

By the standards of the time Butler's punishments were firm but mostly fair; sometimes they could even be administered with a twinkle in his eye if he had some sympathy for the offender's actions. Not infrequently, boys would be sent home with a note to say that they would not be allowed back until they had apologised for their actions. In this way he managed to keep parents involved in the school and on his side.

Discipline was important, but it was the way that the teaching was organised that was revolutionary. Before Butler's time, examinations were rare outside the universities. He introduced six-monthly exams in the school, with positions in class dependent on the results of these. He himself mostly taught the fifth and sixth forms, but each week he examined one of the younger classes in turn to ascertain for himself how the pupils were progressing

Shrewsbury schoolroom, which also served as the chapel, by artist C.W. Radclyffe. (Shrewsbury Museums Service)

academically. In addition, he had weekly conferences with the other masters concerning the boys' progress, both in and out of school. In this way he was able to compile a report on each boy with a mark at the end of each month. From these reports he awarded monthly 'merit money' for those who excelled, and consequently his influence was felt throughout the school.

Such was the success of this regime that former pupils of the school won a quite disproportionate number of prizes at Oxford and Cambridge. As a result, the other public schools were stirred to find out the reason for his success. The headmaster of Harrow even came to sit in on some lessons, and Butler corresponded with the masters at Eton. Soon, these schools and others were following many of his practices, though they baulked at the idea of 'merit money'. Yet beyond all this, Butler himself had that special 'something' which is the hallmark of the outstanding teacher. He treated the older boys almost as equals, developing lifelong friendships with some. He also had an ability to share his enthusiasm for the classics with his pupils, even to the extent of making many of them 'believe that Latin and Greek were the only things worth living for.'[32] Charles Darwin, though, did not thrive on this type of education. He was a thinker and dreamer. He needed to learn things through a process of observation, thinking and experimentation.

6

'THE LARGEST MAN WHOM I EVER SAW'[1]

While Charles was struggling with the challenges of school life, his father Robert was trying to come to terms with his wife's unexpected death. Mostly he seems to have done this by throwing himself even more into his medical work. In tandem with this, his ever more complex financial dealing would take up an increasing amount of his time and energy over the ensuing three decades. These activities provided the backdrop to all of the lives of the Shrewsbury Darwins, so we will consider them in some detail shortly.

If medicine and money were what mostly occupied Robert Darwin, eating provided some solace for the lonely middle-aged man suddenly deprived of his best friend, who had 'entered zealously into all her husband's pursuits'.[2] Overeating was a family failing, in which Robert's father Erasmus indulged to the full, and which Erasmus did not discourage in his children. One writer recalled that, 'Erasmus … had great faith in the instincts of even the human child, enfeebled and vitiated as they are supposed to have been by civilisation. His plan was to let his children eat and drink what they liked; so they ate much fruit and drank bowls of cream.'[3]

So Robert was 'a great feeder, and, it was said, could eat a goose as easily as other men do a partridge'.[4] The story may be apocryphal, but it was remembered that he used to describe a goose 'as a foolish bird – too much for one [to eat], and not enough for two'.[5] His favourite dish was goose pie, which had the following recipe:

> Bone a large goose, then a chicken. Stuff [the chicken] inside the goose, and stuff a pickled tongue inside the chicken and place in a high standing pie crust sprinkled with Beaton Mace pepper and half a pound of butter.[6]

The result of all the 'feeding' was that the tall, slim, young man who had arrived in Shrewsbury 'gay and blooming as a morn of summer',[7] had now become a middle-aged man of enormous proportions. Charles explained that his father was very tall for the times (6ft 2in) and broad shouldered, and that when he had last weighed himself he was twenty-four stone, 'but afterward increased much in weight'.[8] Robert Darwin was very keen on weighing his patients, so presumably the reason he did not weigh himself after he reached twenty-four stone was that his scales did not go above that value.[9] Much later in life he lost a good deal of weight, so that on his eightieth birthday (30 May 1846) he weighed twenty-two stone 3½lb.[10]

In these days, when people are much taller than in the early nineteenth century and obesity is common, it is hard to imagine the impact that such a large man had on his contemporaries. One wrote, 'Dr Darwin was, I think, the biggest man I ever saw out of a show … When he entered the room it was like the door coming upon you broadside on. But what most struck me was the small soft voice that proceeded from this mountain.'[11] His size certainly made him stand out from the crowd, no bad thing for a doctor who could use his bulk as a form of advertising!

His immense size required certain adjustments to his arrangements, especially when he visited people in their homes. He had a carriage specially built for his needs, which was a Brougham with a low step and capacious interior. The other problem in doing home visits was the narrow and often rickety stairs that he had to negotiate to see people in their bedrooms. It was recalled that:

> [It] required some contrivance to facilitate the 'descent of man' and his ascent, as he took his daily rounds. I was told by a lady friend who knew him well that he usually descended the stairs backwards, and never failed to express his admiration of her broad stairs of oak with its massive hand rails, which afforded him ample security. My friend was once showing him the way up to the room of a patient in her house, when he said, 'Now will you run up first like a light post coach, and I will follow like a broad-wheeled wagon.' I have been assured that he would not venture to ascend the stairs in some houses, which were very narrow and flimsily built, but would stand at the bottom enquiring the symptoms of the sick patient, and dictate in his singularly high-pitched and somewhat squeaking voice, the diet and treatment he considered necessary.[12]

On other occasions his coachman Mark Briggs had to go before the doctor to test floors and stairs to see if they would stand his weight.[13]

Silhouette of Robert Darwin – date and artist unknown. (Shrewsbury Museums Service)

It is surprising that Robert Darwin's obesity seems to have had little impact on his longevity, since he lived to the age of eighty-two. Perhaps one reason was that, like his father, he was virtually teetotal. Although he did not drink alcohol, he liked port or sherry in his sauces and gravies, because, he said,

The Doctor's gate. (Author's collection)

'Wine requires cooking.'[14] The control of alcohol intake was an important part of his advice to patients, advice that must have been of benefit to many.

In addition to avoiding alcohol, he tried to take some exercise, such as walking to meetings of the Trustees of Millington's Hospital, whose board he joined in January 1807.[15] The journey required him to walk right down to Frankwell at the bottom of the hill and then ascend the other side, a distance of nearly a mile. He served as a trustee until the end of his life, and such was the esteem in which he was held, that the other trustees made a special gate in the wall of the hospital to enable him, as he grew older, to have to walk only across the road to attend meetings.[16] This 'doctor's gate' can still be seen today.

A suspicion that his health may have been affected by his obesity concerns an illness he suffered in 1829. Charles Darwin wrote to his cousin:

> My father has been very ill, but is now I hope steadily but slowly getting better. The cause of this illness is a deep-seated Erysipelus [sic] in his neck, attended with a great deal of fever. I am afraid he has undergone a great deal of suffering, and that it will be some time before he quite recovers the

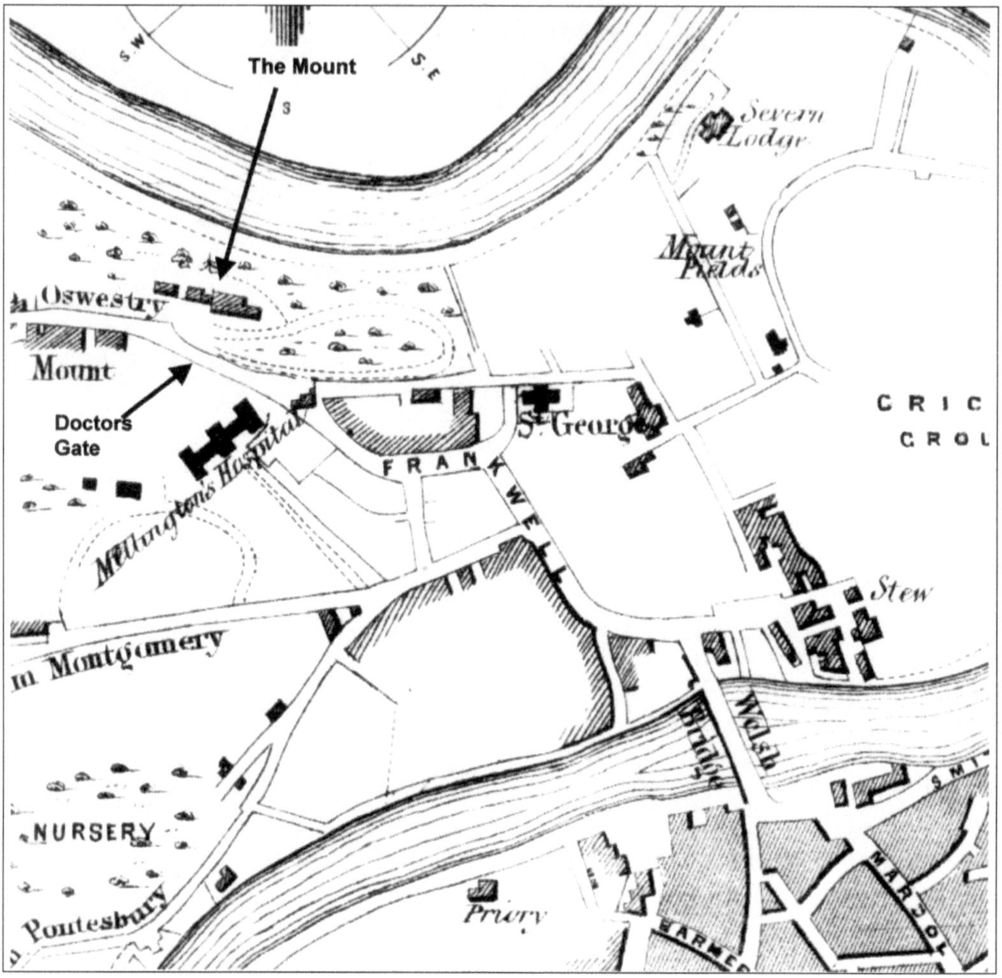

Map of The Mount showing the position of the Doctor's gate. (Henry Pidgeon, *Memorials of Shrewsbury* J.H. Leake, Shrewsbury, 1850)

> effect of it. I should have gone down to Shrewsbury, only that his medical attendants particularly insisted that he should be kept as quiet as possible. My sisters appear to have been terribly alarmed, as I suppose on Wednesday he was in imminent danger.[17]

Charles' description of 'deep-seated erysipelas in his neck' strongly suggests that Robert Darwin had a carbuncle, a notoriously deep-seated abscess in the back of the neck, which could easily have been fatal in pre-antibiotic days. Today, this condition is often associated with poorly controlled type 2 diabetes, usually brought on by obesity and excessive sugar consumption. Diabetes of this sort was unknown to the doctors of the time, but, if he suffered from it, Robert Darwin's weight loss in later life could well have improved the situation without him realising it.

This illness increased his daughters' pressure on him to scale back his medical work. So, on 3 February 1831, just before his sixty-fifth birthday, he resigned as physician to the Salop Infirmary.[18] This is a cue to retrace our steps in time and see how he practised as a doctor.

7

'KNOWN TO EVERY MAN, WOMAN AND CHILD ...'[1]

Six months before Charles Darwin left Shrewsbury School, on 9 November 1824 to be precise, his eldest sister Marianne was married at St Chad's Church, Shrewsbury. Her husband was Dr Henry Parker, and at the age of thirty-six he was ten years older than his bride. Like Robert Darwin he had graduated as an MD from Edinburgh University, and it appears that soon after he qualified in 1814 he began to practise at Overton, just over the Welsh border from Shropshire, in the County of Flint.[2] Doubtless it was because he was a medical neighbour of Robert Darwin's that the two soon became acquainted. Perhaps it was at one of the Darwin's 'great feasts' that he first met Marianne?

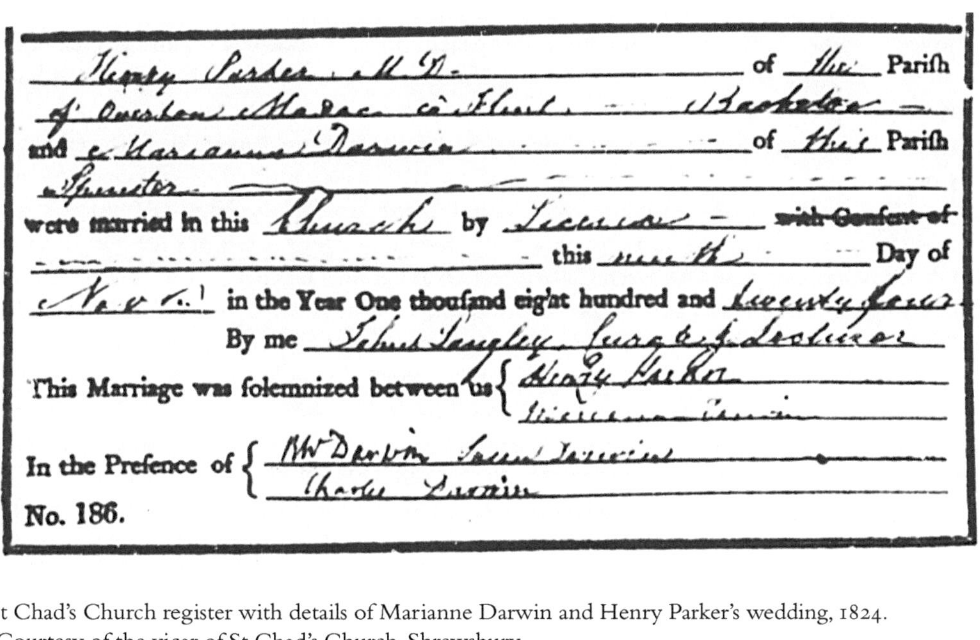
Henry Parker M.D. of the Parish of Overton Maelor co. Flint Bachelor and Marianne Darwin of this Parish Spinster were married in this Church by Licence ~~with Confent of~~ this ninth Day of Novr in the Year One thoufand eight hundred and twenty four

By me John Langley Curate

This Marriage was folemnized between us { Henry Parker, Marianne Darwin

In the Prefence of { RW Darwin, Susan Darwin, Charles Darwin

No. 186.

St Chad's Church register with details of Marianne Darwin and Henry Parker's wedding, 1824. (Courtesy of the vicar of St Chad's Church, Shrewsbury.

The Brow, Overton, home of Henry and Marianne Parker. (Author's collection)

The signatures on the marriage register may provide a clue as to the characters of the newly-weds.[3] Henry's signature is bold and clear, while Marianne's is tiny and seems to disappear. The latter tends to confirm the impression that Marianne was diffident and retiring. One oddity with the marriage was the witnesses. Unsurprisingly, Robert Darwin signed first, and Susan Darwin signed as another family representative. The third witness was the fifteen-year old Charles – why he should sign as well, and why there was no witness from the Parker side of the family, is a mystery.

The Parkers settled at The Brow, a converted farmhouse on the edge of Overton, with magnificent views over the River Dee, which was their home for the rest of their lives. It took a while for Marianne's youngest sister, Catherine, to like her new brother-in-law,[4] but the Parkers quickly became an integral part of the Darwin family circle. The couple soon had their hands full with the arrival of four sons and a daughter over the next twelve years. Robert, affectionately known as 'Parky' by the rest of the family, was the oldest, being born in 1825. Henry junior followed two years after. Frank (born 1829) was third in line, while Charles was born in 1831. Mary, the much longed-for daughter, was born in 1836. The Darwins and the Parkers frequently visited each other. One such occasion was the time when Robert had scarlet fever so severely that he couldn't be moved from his boarding school in Oswestry, so Marianne went into school to nurse him. But Marianne was pregnant and exhausted, so Caroline went to Overton to help her, while the three younger boys stayed at the Mount with Susan and Catherine.[5]

Like his father-in-law, Henry Parker had a large and successful practice, which included a good number of the influential families of the area. It has been suggested that Robert Darwin

Dr Robert Darwin – W.W. Ouless' copy of an original by J.C. Pardon. (Shrewsbury Museums Service)

took him on as a partner,[6] but there is no documentary evidence for this. It is more likely that while Robert Darwin was active in practice they had an informal working relationship (perhaps covering for each other's absences, for example), but that when Robert wound down his practice after 1831 most of his patients were transferred to the care of his son-in-law. Henry was well known and respected in Shropshire, being elected unanimously as a physician at the Salop Infirmary in 1846. The proposer, Col Wingfield of Onslow Hall, stated that 'Dr Parker [was] a gentleman of highly honourable principles and amiable qualities ... well known to many gentlemen ... 'The seconder, Robert Burton of Longner Hall, said that Dr Parker possessed 'eminent skill, constant attention to his duties, and truly Christian charity.' Mr Burton added that he had been acquainted with Dr Parker for over thirty years.[7]

At the time of acquiring his son-in-law, Robert Darwin was at the height of his fame. He had been in practice for nearly forty years, and it was said that 'his yellow chaise, [with] his burly form and countenance within, were known to every man, woman and child over a wide extent of country'.[8] He always wore the same clothes, designed to convey the impression of a successful, yet unostentatious, professional man. His three-piece suit (coat, waistcoat and breeches) was made of snuff-coloured cloth, as were his gaiters, which were buttoned above the knee. His waistcoat had an old-fashioned flap (or lappet) above the pockets, into one of which disappeared a conspicuous watch-chain. His shirt was frilled, according to the fashion, and his attire was completed with a many-folded linen necktie.[9]

His workload was phenomenal. Mornings were mostly taken up with seeing patients at home and attending to his correspondence, since many consultations were by letter, and other doctors and apothecaries also solicited his advice by the same means. An insight into this type of consultation is preserved in the following letter, whose date and recipient (evidently a titled lady) is lost. Robert obviously composed the letter in a hurry, while he was stopping off on the way to another visit. He wrote:

> I received your ladyship's letter ... You may be assured the pain you mention does not proceed from any affection of the chest you fear. It certainly is caused by phlem [sic], and if that is not caused by stress, it is by bile in the [?] or wind in the stomach – certainly [double underlined] not by fluid in the chest ... in addition to what you are now doing, I wish you would apply 6 leeches to the stomach (or rather the right side of the stomach) and afterwards a blister.[10]

Each letter would take time and care to compose – if he said the wrong thing he might lose a lucrative patient, which may be why he added that he considered her letter 'a fresh proof of the confidence you have in me ... '

Once the patients had been seen at home (no appointments in those days), the visits would begin. He would squeeze himself into his bright yellow chaise, and go to all points of the compass. He kept a notebook as an aide-memoire of what he had given to some of those he visited.[11] Selecting the pages for 1818-24 at random we find him visiting Ellesmere, Wem, Myddle, Hordley and Whittington in the north of the county; Newport, Tern Hall and Broseley in the east; Kemberton, Millichope, Homer and Ludlow in the south; and Brockton in the west. Over the Welsh border he visited Pool (Welshpool), Talgarth (between Machynlleth and Aberdovey) and Llanidloes, and in the opposite direction he went to Stafford. From other sources we know he saw patients in Lichfield,[12] Birmingham[13] and Herefordshire.[14] Sometimes he did 'branch surgeries' at suitable inns – the Lion (presumably Shrewsbury), the Talbot (probably the one in Market Street, Shrewsbury, or it could be an inn of the same name at Atcham or Ruyton XI Towns), and the Tontine (in Ironbridge) are mentioned in the period 1818-24. He was also the unofficial doctor to many of his wider family and friends, especially the Wedgwoods of Maer Hall, and also his stepmother in Derbyshire, whom he had to visit on occasions.[15] Even members of the immediate family were recorded in his notebook; for example, Marianne and Caroline were treated on 24 November 1818. Day or night, in all weathers, he might have to be on the road.[16] Driving over country lanes would be exhausting at the best of times; in adverse weather conditions it must have required an iron constitution to

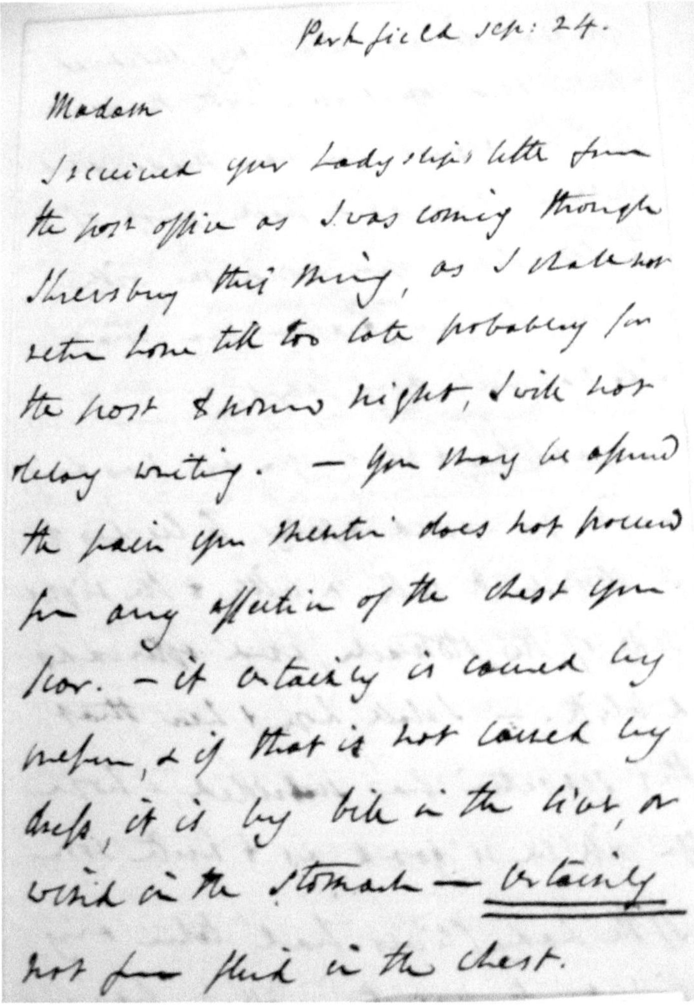

Parkfield Sep: 24.

Madam

I received your Ladyship's letter from the post office as I was coming through Shrewsbury this morning, as I shall not return home till too late probably for the post tomorrow night, I will not delay writing. — You may be assured the pain you mention does not proceed from any affection of the chest you fear. — it certainly is caused by [illegible], & if that is not caused by [illegible], it is by bile in the liver, or wind in the stomach — certainly not from fluid in the chest.

Letter from Dr Robert Darwin to a patient. Date and recipient unknown. (Shropshire Archives)

survive. The visiting workload troubled Susannah at times. She wrote to her brother:

> The Dr [Robert] is not in very good feather just at present; he is so much engaged that it harasses him a good deal. Surely warmer weather must come soon, and that, I hope, will give him more liberty. He is gone 7 miles beyond Whitechurch [Whitchurch, North Shropshire], which is out of his usual beat.[17]

Because his notebook is not a precise record of all his consultations, but rather an aide memoire to help him the next time he saw the patient, it is hard to know how many consultations he did. In the period 1818-24 there are records of around 7,000 home visits, making at least 1,000 a year. Many people are mentioned repeatedly, indicating that in times of crisis he may have visited the same person frequently. The convention of the day was often to spend a significant amount of time, even a night or more, with the patient, especially if they were of the upper classes, so Robert certainly earned his money.

Who were these people who made his working life so busy? The short answer is that they were from every part of society. His notebooks read like a 'who's who' of the rich and

Weston Park, 1891, which Robert Darwin visited to treat the family of the Earl of Bradford. (Shrewsbury Museums Service)

famous. There was the Earl of Stanford (presumably on a visit to the county), and the Corbets, a many-branched family who had owned great tracts of land since the Norman Conquest. The Humffreys' family seat was near Llanfyllin, then in Montgomeryshire. They were near neighbours to the Powis dynasty, whose home is now a noted National Trust property. Robert also travelled to the extreme east of the county to visit the Earl of Bradford at Weston Park, and to Cleobury Mortimer in the far south of Shropshire to treat the Childe family. Nearer to Shrewsbury, Robert looked after various branches of the famous Hill family.[18] Less aristocratic, but powerful through their mining and iron-founding interests, were the Botfields, who lived in what is now the Telford area. The Salts and Pembertons were two influential legal families, and the Blunts were one of the main chemists in Shrewsbury.

These patients, and others like them, were the people Robert Darwin needed to cultivate to keep his earnings high. Alongside them the notebooks also list dozens of others who are not now remembered. Presumably they were lesser landowners, farmers, tradesmen and the like. This group of patients provided his bread and butter income. Those who are not mentioned in his notebooks were the poor, who could barely afford a bottle of medicine, far less the services of such a grand physician, unless he was to treat them for free. And this he did, both through his appointment at the hospital, and also by seeing the poor at his surgery at The Mount or visiting them in their homes. In this he was not unique, for treating the poor for free was something other physicians of the time were willing to do. Charles recalled what happened when his father offered this service:

> For the benefit of the district in which he lived Dr Darwin offered to dispense medicine

> gratis to any one who applied and was not able to pay. He was surprised to find that very few of the sick poor availed themselves of his offer, and guessing that the reason must have been a dislike of becoming the recipients of charity, he devised a plan to neutralise this feeling. Whenever any poor persons applied for medical aid, he told them that he would supply the medicine, but that they must pay for the bottles. This little distinction made all the difference, and ever afterwards the poor used to flock to the doctor's house for relief as a matter of right.[19]

It has also been said that, on occasion, if a patient gave him a fee and he did not feel they could afford it, he would take the coin with one hand and return it with the other to save them losing face. Not only did he give his time and medicines free, but he also gave practical help for the poor. One of those he helped was a Mrs Cook. Her story is explained in the following extract:

> Dr Robert Darwin had a taste for mechanical invention, like his father Erasmus Darwin. He made a design for a nursery lamp, for use in feeding children. It was in part manufactured at Etruria [the Wedgwood pottery], and had a large sale. [Robert Darwin] confined the sale of this in Shrewsbury to some dealers in earthenware, of the name of Cook, who were poor and needed assistance. Of [Robert's] kindness Mrs Cook thus wrote to Mr Byerley at Etruria in January 1804 ... 'Many trials I have been called to pass through, but none so severe as the loss of my truly valuable and beloved husband, Thomas Cook. This painful event took place on September 4th, after an illness of five months, all [of] which time Dr Darwin attended him with a tender solicitude peculiar to himself, and which I hope will ever be remembered by me with the utmost gratitude. Not only was this attendance gratis [free], but wine, fruit, peas, artichokes etc. sent frequently from his house ... [20]

As well as the rich and the poor, Robert Darwin had a flourishing practice with children, whom he loved. Perhaps unusually for the time, he spoke to them directly, not just to the parents. A contemporary recalled that 'he would address them in his small, high-pitched, falsetto voice, and if their answers pleased him he would reply. And occasionally, lifting them on to a chair or table, he would measure their heads with his broad hand, as though reading character, and mentally prognosticating their future fate.'[21] (The writer is explaining that Robert Darwin followed the then popular fashion of phrenology – a belief that one could ascertain mental faculties from the shape of the skull.) Children seemed to love and respond to him. For example, one John Aston still remembered a consultation with him over eighty years before,[22] and another contemporary recalled children in the houses near The Mount standing at their doors weeping on the day of his death.[23]

In addition to all of these people, Robert was the person many of the wider family turned to when they were ill. An example of this was Catherine (Kitty) Wedgwood, Susannah's sister, who became so seriously ill in 1823 that she and her sister Sarah moved to The Mount to be under Robert's constant care.[24] In the event, Kitty suffered a long and painful terminal illness, and died in the August of the same year. Afterwards, Sarah wrote to her brother Jos, 'I hope Marianne and Caroline will bear it [her death] pretty well. They have nursed her with heroical fortitude ... The Doctor has had great fatigue, he expects a long sound sleep tonight, which I hope he will have ... '[25]

8

'A REMARKABLE MAN'[1]

An insight into the sort of conditions that Robert Darwin and Henry Parker treated at the Salop Infirmary is given by an overview of the diagnosis of patients seen in the year 1845-6.[2] What immediately strikes one as unexpected is that the largest diagnostic category was syphilis, and that 'prostitutes', all of whom had syphilis, are listed as an occupation. The other main diagnoses were what one would expect – top of the list being dyspepsia, injuries, chronic arthritis, and ulcers (presumably of the leg in men and women such as agricultural labourers and domestic servants who were on their feet all day). Patients with infectious diseases, except tuberculosis (then called phthisis), were rarely admitted to the hospital because of the fear of cross-infection. A diagnosis of heart disease, diabetes or tumour was uncommon. Virtually all the diagnostic categories (except perhaps 'hysteria', 'hypochondriasis' and 'chlorosis') are similar to those used by the modern doctor, though some of the diagnostic categories are quite broad.

In this diagnostic process the observation by the doctor was critical, and Robert Darwin was recognised as a master of the art. Charles Darwin wrote that, 'the sharpness of his observation led him to predict with remarkable skill the course of any illness, and he suggested endless small details of relief … Long before typhoid fever was recognised as distinct, my father told me that two utterly distinct kinds of illness were confounded under the name of typhus fever.'[3] (The two diseases were confused because they may have a similar rash, but are caused by different organisms transmitted in different ways.)

The patients that Robert Darwin saw either at home or in his surgery were suffering from a wider range of illnesses than those seen at the infirmary. He kept his own list of treatments for various diseases, which he carefully recorded.[4] Sometimes his diagnosis is one that a modern doctor would understand – dropsy [heart failure], gonorrhoea, persistent abortion [miscarriage], jaundice, puerperal [post-natal] fever and piles are typical examples. At other times he merely described symptoms without any attempt to make a 'modern' diagnosis. Examples of this are 'costiveness [constipation] with debility and a pale face', 'dry cough without fever', 'eruption of the skin' and 'slight bilious complaints'. As we saw in an earlier chapter, he treated mental as well as physical complaints (for example, he had a treatment for 'nervous and hysterical neurosis'). He also had to attend in cases of suicide, though there was no formal inquiry then into the cause of death.[5] He treated women for pregnancy-related complaints (such as 'opening pills

A Statistical Table of Diseases, &c. of In-Patients admitted into the Salop Infirmary, between Midsummer, 1845, and Midsummer, 1846:—arranged by Mr. Samuel Wood, House Surgeon.

	Diseases of the Respiratory Organs.				Diseases of the Circulation.		Diseases of the Digestive Organs.					Diseases of the Nervous System.							Diseases Reproductive	
	Bronchitis.	Pneumonia.	Pleuritis.	Phthisis.	Diseases of the Heart.	Hemorrhage.	Dyspepsia.	Diabetes.	Hepatic Disease.	Diarrhoea.	Hernia.	Hypochondriasis.	Hysteria.	Chorea.	Delirium Tremens.	Apoplexy, &c.	Paralysis.	Curvature.	Amenorrhoea and Chlorosis.	Menorrhagia.
Agricul. Labourers	23	..	..	12	3	1	31	..	14	3	3	2	..	..	2	2	3	1	..	..
Bakers	..	..	..	..	..	..	..	..	..	..	..	..	..	..	..	..	1	..	..	..
Blacksmiths and Moulders	..	..	1	1	2	..	2	..	1	..	..	..	..	..	1	1	1	..	..	..
Booksellers	..	..	..	..	..	..	..	..	..	..	..	..	..	..	..	..	..	..	..	..
Bricklayers and Masons	1	..	..	1	1	..	..	..	..	..	..	..	..	..	..	..	..	..	..	..
Butchers	..	..	..	1	..	..	1	..	..	..	..	..	..	..	..	..	..	..	..	..
Carpenters and Sawyers	1	..	..	..	..	..	1	..	..	..	..	..	..	..	..	..	1	..	..	..
Children	..	..	..	..	..	..	..	..	..	..	..	..	..	4	..	..	..	1	..	..
Chimney Sweepers	..	..	..	..	..	..	..	..	..	..	..	..	..	..	..	..	..	..	..	..
Domestics	1	1	..	4	1	1	10	..	6	1	2	2	3	..	..	..	4	..	..	..
Dressmakers	..	..	..	..	1	..	..	..	..	..	..	..	1	..	..	..	1	..	1	1
Factory Weavers &c	2	..	..	..	..	..	1	..	..	..	..	2	..	..	..	..	1	1	..	..
Gardeners	2	..	..	..	..	..	1	..	..	..	..	..	..	..	..	..	..	..	..	..
Hairdressers	..	..	..	1	..	..	..	..	..	..	..	..	..	..	..	..	..	..	..	..
Hawkers	..	..	..	..	..	..	..	..	..	..	..	..	..	..	..	..	..	..	..	..
Miners & Colliers	3	..	..	3	..	..	4	..	..	..	..	1	..	..	..	..	1	..	..	..
Prostitutes	..	..	..	..	..	..	..	..	..	..	..	..	..	..	..	..	..	..	..	..
Quarry-men and Stone-cutters	.	..	..	..	..	..	..	..	..	..	..	..	..	..	..	..	..	..	..	..
Servants (Female)	5	..	..	9	1	1	30	2	6	2	..	..	12	..	..	..	..	2	48	..
Ditto (Male)	3	..	..	6	..	0	9	..	..	..	..	..	..	..	1	..	..	1	..	..
Shoemakers	3	..	..	2	..	1	•3	..	1	..	..	..	..	..	..	..	..	..	..	..
Soldiers and Pensioners	1	..	..	..	..	..	..	..	..	..	..	..	..	..	..	..	..	..	..	..
Tailors	4	..	..	1	..	..	1	..	..	..	..	..	..	..	..	..	..	..	..	..
Tinmen	..	..	..	..	..	..	..	..	..	..	..	..	..	..	..	..	1	..	..	..
Writing Clerks	.	..	..	..	..	..	..	..	..	..	..	..	..	..	..	..	..	..	..	..
	49	1	1	41	9	4	94	2	28	6	5	7	16	4	4	3	14	6	49	1
AGES.																				
Under 10 years	..	..	..	..	..	..	..	..	..	..	..	..	..	1	..	..	..	..	..	..
Above 10, under 20	6	..	1	12	3	1	8	..	6	1	..	1	5	3	..	..	2	4	30	..
.... 20, ... 30	11	..	..	13	3	1	34	1	6	2	1	2	9	..	..	2	3	2	18	1
.... 30, ... 40	10	..	..	7	2	1	18	1	8	1	1	3	2	.	2	1	1	..	1	..
.... 40, ... 50	12	1	..	8	1	1	15	..	3	1	2	1	..	..	2	..	4	..	..	..
.... 50, ... 60	9	..	..	1	..	..	14	..	5	1	1	..	..	..	..	..	3	..	..	..
.... 60, ... 70	..	..	..	..	..	..	4	..	..	..	..	..	..	..	..	..	1	..	..	..
.... 70, ... 80	1	..	..	..	..	..	1	..	..	..	..	..	..	..	..	..	..	..	..	..
.... 80, ... 90	..	..	..	..	..	..	..	..	..	..	..	..	..	..	..	..	..	..	..	..
	49	1	1	41	9	4	94	2	28	6	5	7	16	4	4	3	14	6	49	1

	of the Organs.										Diseases of Uncertain and Variable Seat.													
	Diseases of the Uterus.	Ovarian Dropsy.	Stricture.	Hydrocele.	Ascites.	Diseases of the Skin.	Ditto of the Eye.	Ditto of the Bones & Joints.	Fractures and Dislocations.	Injuries.	Acute Rheumatism.	Chronic Ditto.	Fevers.	Scrofula.	Cancer.	Malignant Diseases.	Debility.	Tumours.	Deformities.	Ulcers.	Fistula.	Abscesses and Local Inflammations.	Syphilis.	Totals.
Agricul. Labourers	..	..	6	12	4	5	14	13	23	46	3	44	18	8	3	4	2	10	3	32	5	15	23	393
Bakers	..	..	..	..	..	..	..	..	..	..	..	..	..	..	..	..	..	..	..	..	..	..	..	1
Blacksmiths and Moulders	..	..	..	..	..	..	1	1	..	5	..	5	..	1	..	..	..	..	..	..	..	..	4	27
Booksellers	..	..	..	..	..	..	..	..	..	..	..	..	..	..	..	..	..	..	1	..	..	..	..	1
Bricklayers and Masons	..	..	1	..	..	..	1	1	..	2	1	..	1	..	..	..	..	..	1	..	..	..	4	15
Butchers	..	..	..	..	..	..	1	..	..	..	..	1	..	..	..	..	..	..	..	..	..	..	2	6
Carpenters and Sawyers	..	..	..	1	..	..	..	2	..	2	1	4	..	1	..	..	1	..	..	4	..	1	5	25
Children	..	..	..	1	..	..	4	8	3	10	..	4	1	11	..	..	..	3	1	..	..	5	..	56
Chimney Sweepers	..	..	..	..	..	..	..	..	..	..	..	..	..	..	..	..	..	..	..	..	..	..	1	1
Domestics	6	1	..	..	1	..	1	2	2	6	..	9	2	2	4	3	..	4	..	15	1	5	3	103
Dressmakers	..	..	..	..	..	..	..	..	..	..	..	..	..	..	..	..	..	..	..	..	1	1	1	8
Factory Weavers &c	..	..	..	..	..	..	2	1	..	1	..	..	1	1	..	..	..	1	..	3	..	4	6	27
Gardeners	..	..	..	..	..	..	..	..	1	..	..	..	..	..	..	..	..	..	..	1	..	..	1	6
Hairdressers	..	..	..	..	..	..	..	..	..	..	..	..	..	..	..	..	..	..	..	..	..	..	..	1
Hawkers	..	..	..	..	..	..	..	..	..	..	..	..	..	..	..	..	..	..	..	..	..	..	2	2
Miners & Colliers	..	..	1	1	..	..	3	2	..	5	..	3	..	1	..	..	..	1	..	..	1	2	6	38
Prostitutes	..	..	..	..	..	..	..	..	..	..	..	..	..	..	..	..	..	..	..	..	..	..	21	21
Quarry-men and Stone-cutters	..	..	..	..	..	..	..	..	..	..	..	1	..	..	..	..	..	..	..	..	..	..	..	1
Servants (Female)	.	2	..	..	..	2	4	6	1	7	2	10	9	7	2	..	1	2	1	24	..	22	4	224
Ditto (Male)	..	..	..	..	..	1	4	1	4	4	1	5	3	..	..	..	..	..	1	2	..	2	5	53
Shoemakers	..	..	5	3	..	..	1	..	..	..	..	..	1	1	..	..	..	..	..	..	..	3	5	29
Soldiers and Pensioners	..	..	..	..	..	..	..	..	..	..	..	1	..	..	..	..	..	..	..	..	..	..	2	4
Tailors	..	..	..	..	..	..	1	..	2	..	..	..	2	..	..	..	..	..	..	..	..	1	2	14
Tinmen	..	..	..	..	..	..	..	..	..	..	.	..	..	..	..	..	..	..	..	..	..	..	..	1
Writing Clerks	..	..	..	..	..	..	..	1	..	..	..	..	..	..	..	..	..	1	..	..	..	..	..	2
	6	3	13	18	5	8	37	38	36	88	8	87	38	33	9	7	4	22	8	81	8	61	97	1059
AGES.																								
Under 10 years	..	..	..	1	..	..	..	2	1	4	..	..	..	6	..	..	..	1	2	1	..	5	..	24
Above 10, under 20	..	1	..	5	..	2	14	15	15	23	3	12	12	14	1	..	..	4	3	9	..	22	31	269
.... 20, ... 30	1	2	3	1	..	1	9	13	4	20	4	25	14	6	..	..	..	5	1	29	2	14	56	319
.... 30, ... 40	2	..	4	1	2	2	4	4	5	11	1	16	4	5	1	2	2	5	1	11	2	8	7	159
.... 40, ... 50	3	..	4	6	1	2	2	1	1	12	..	14	3	2	1	2	..	2	1	9	3	10	2	132
.... 50, ... 60	..	..	2	3	..	1	6	..	8	6	..	11	2	..	1	3	..	3	..	12	1	1	1	95
.... 60, ... 70	..	..	.	1	2	..	1	2	2	6	..	9	3	..	3	..	1	2	..	5	..	1	..	43
.... 70, ... 80	..	..	..	..	..	..	1	1	..	5	..	..	..	..	2	..	1	..	..	5	..	..	..	17
.... 80, ... 90	..	..	..	..	.	..	..	..	..	1	..	..	..	..	..	..	..	..	..	..	..	..	..	1
	6	3	13	18	5	8	37	38	36	88	8	87	38	33	9	7	4	22	8	81	8	61	97	1059

Details of inpatients at the Salop Infirmary 1845-46. (Shropshire Archives) taken during pregnancy'), but did not attend confinements, leaving that to the 'man midwives'. ('Man midwives' were surgeons with experience of obstetrics.[6]) Sometimes, Robert Darwin's cases were emergencies, such as haemorrhages[7] or nosebleeds.[8]

Having made some sort of diagnosis, which in itself can be therapeutic, how was the consultation to proceed? One of the most important treatment tools available to the doctor is his or her own personality, and if this is so today, how much more was this true 200 years ago! Sometimes, all that Robert Darwin and his contemporaries had to offer their desperate patients was their presence and support. So Robert's success as a doctor was due in no small part to his personality, which contained an interesting mixture of traits.

As we have already seen, he was often strong and forceful, so much so that he offended some patients. Charles described one such:

> I remember my father telling us one day with a laugh, that several persons had asked him whether Miss Piggott (a grand old lady in Shropshire) had called on him, so that at last he enquired why they asked him. He was told that Miss Piggott, whom my father had somehow mortally offended, was telling everybody that she would call and tell, 'that fat old doctor very plainly what she thought of him'. She had already called, but her courage had failed, and no one could have been more courteous and friendly![9]

But the force of his personality could be used as a form of therapy. Charles continued,

> As a boy I went to stay at the house of Major B, whose wife was insane; and the poor creature, as soon as she saw me, was in the most abject state of terror that I ever saw, weeping bitterly and asking me over and over again, 'Is your father coming?' But [she] was soon pacified. On my return home I asked my father why she was so frightened, and he answered he was very glad to hear it, as he had frightened her on purpose. He felt sure that she could be kept in safety and much happier without any restraint if her husband could influence her, whenever she became at all violent, by proposing to send for Dr Darwin. These words succeeded perfectly during the rest of her long life.[10]

However, his strong and forthright way of speaking, especially when he pronounced the patient to be terminally ill, might cause offence to those who cared for the patient. Charles described one relative who summoned up the courage to explain the need for Robert to be less abrasive.

> My father told a lady that her husband would certainly die. Some months afterwards he saw the widow, who was a very sensible woman, and she said, 'You are a very young man, and allow me to advise you always to give, as long as you possibly can, hope to any near relation nursing a patient. You made me despair, and I lost strength.' My father said that he had often since seen the paramount importance, for the sake of the patient, of keeping up the hope and with it the strength of the nurse in charge.[11]

Robert did not always find his own advice easy to follow! A correspondent writing in the newspaper remembered that, 'kind as he undoubtedly was, he occasionally pronounced the fate of his patients in such as abrupt and positive manner that all hope of recovery was at once dispelled.' The writer then went on to tell a personal anecdote to illustrate this:

> My wife's mother was suffering in an advanced stage of consumption [tuberculosis], and on what

> happened to be his last visit to her [Dr Darwin] said to her husband in a quick and decided manner, 'Your wife, Mr H, is a dead woman, a dead woman; she cannot live more than a fortnight!' She died a very few days afterwards. Some people were much offended by this manner, and called in another doctor.[12]

Another lady remembered that:

> A young female friend of hers, whom Dr Darwin was attending at her house, was pronounced by him to be in a hopeless state, and he said she would be dead in a day or two. But the friends of the young person, being hurt and offended, called in Dr Dugard, who at once altered the treatment, giving her nourishing food and abundant stimulants, and then bled her, by which means she slightly rallied for a time. Dr Darwin called shortly afterwards, and enquired from the servant, not offering to go in, at what time the young woman died. 'Died, sir,' exclaimed the maid, 'why, she is wonderfully better! Dr Dugard has been and given her physic [medicine], and she is much improved.' The doctor entered his carriage and drove away without another word. Dr Darwin anticipated modern practice by discarding bleeding, and the case of this young woman confirmed his judgment, for a relapse immediately followed, and she passed away.[13]

This incident illustrates the competition in that era between doctors. Dr DuGard's income presumably derived entirely from his medical practice, so, for fear of losing money and reputation, he had to appear to be doing something for the patient, even though he too may have thought that the case was hopeless. Robert, on the other hand, was willing to speak the truth, knowing that his finances and reputation were secure, though he could have done it in a more kindly way.

But it was not just the force of his personality that made Robert successful as a doctor. As with his diagnostic skill, he had what seemed at times an almost supernatural knack of reading people's characters and motives. He often did not understand how it happened, but it is likely to have been a combination of sensitivity towards the feelings of others, allied to acute observation and sound common sense. This sensitivity helped his treatment of patients, but it came at a personal cost to himself. He once confided to his son that when he was old he did not like to go out for a drive because, 'every road out of Shrewsbury is associated in my mind with some painful event.'[14] In all probability his abruptness, especially in dealing with painful situations such as breaking bad news, was a way of coping with his own pain when faced with the suffering of others.

He had what we now call intuition, which a modern doctor describes as follows: 'Intuition is hard to put into words, but is a sense that something somehow is just "not right". It is … perhaps a change in the tone, pitch, or pace of [the patient's] voice, or a change in posture. But really intuition is just a feeling … '[15]

Robert honed his consulting skills by long practice. Especially in dealing with women, he realised that often apparently trivial physical complaints were in fact due to unhappiness, usually in marriage. He learned to get to the underlying emotional problem quickly by passing over the physical complaint. He would also encourage a woman to cry rather than ordering her to stop, because he found that this staunched the flow of tears much more quickly. He then could get on with the consultation![16]

He was also aided by a prodigious memory, which doubtless increased the patients' confidence in the apparently all-remembering doctor. Charles recalled:

> My father possessed an extraordinary memory, especially for dates, so that he knew when he was

very old the day of the birth, marriage, and death of a multitude of persons in Shropshire. And he once told me that this power annoyed him, for if he once heard a date he could not forget it, and thus the deaths of his friends were often recalled to mind.[17]

But the characteristic that most endeared him to the majority of his patients was his genuine kindness and sympathy. We have already seen how he not only treated poor patients for free, but he often helped them with small gifts. Charles noted that:

> Of all his characteristic qualities, his sympathy was pre-eminent, and I believe that it was this which made him for a time hate his profession, as it constantly brought suffering before his eyes. Sympathy with the joy of others is a much rarer endowment than sympathy with their pains, and it is no exaggeration to say that to give pleasure to others was to my father an intense pleasure.[18]

Robert's friend William Owen of Woodhouse summed up this side of his character when he wrote, 'There is something about him so liberal, so high minded and yet so unassuming that it is quite impossible to know him well without respecting and loving him.'[19]

Another important duty of the doctor was to provide a prognosis, in which Robert was often spot-on, even if sometimes he was rather brutal with the truth. The problem he found was trying to provide some hope for the patient while avoiding lying. Charles Darwin explained what happened to his father in the case of Robert Pemberton senior (1728-96), who was an attorney and Mayor of Shrewsbury in 1781:[20]

> He was sent for by Mr Pemberton, who said, 'From all that I have seen and heard of you I believe that you are the sort of man who will speak the truth, and if I ask you will tell me when I am dying. Now I much desire that you should attend me, if you will promise, whatever I may say, always to declare that I am not going to die.' My father acquiesced on the understanding that his words should in fact have no meaning.[21]

If his personality was the most powerful therapeutic tool at his disposal, Robert Darwin also tried to use all the other treatments available to him. As we have already seen, he did not bleed his patients. This procedure remained popular with both doctors and patients until well into the nineteenth century, but Robert's patients seem to have accepted that he did not do it, and must have benefited thereby. However, as we saw before, he used leeches, so he didn't dispense entirely with the old ways.

A more modern treatment that Robert Darwin recommended was vaccination to prevent smallpox, which Thomas Telford mentioned in a letter to his friend Matthew Davidson.[22] The herbal and chemical remedies publicly on offer at this time were legion, many of which had exaggerated claims for their effectiveness, as evidenced by the advertisements for them in the press. Robert Darwin seems to have tried to avoid the excesses of these enthusiasts, and he built up his own *materia medica* – substances used to treat illness – 'a choice repertory of the most precious gifts of nature and science', as one authority called them.[23] Robert carefully recorded these treatments, some of which have stood the test of time.[24] These include antacids for indigestion, antiscorbutic plants for scurvy, *digitalis* for heart failure and opiate derivatives for pain. He also had effective emetics (to bring on vomiting) and laxatives, though the modern doctor would quail at the indications for their use. He seems to have been much more conservative than his father in his prescription of opiates and *digitalis*, recognising the importance of using them in the correct dosage. In this, he followed the example of William Withering, who 'pronounced it the physician's duty to withstand the clamour, raised by the sick person and the apothecary, for a deluge of dosing'. Withering contended that patients had to be protected from their own rather naïve assumption that the more medicine they took, the more they were fighting their disorders.[25] Robert Darwin also warned his son Charles against taking arsenic for a skin complaint.[26]

Mention of arsenic reminds us that, while many of the remedies available to Robert Darwin were of herbal origin, chemicals, especially metals in one form or another, were also widely used. These metals included mercury, which was used both internally (when the dosages were often in the toxic range), and on the skin as a caustic. Other metals used were arsenic (as a 'tonic'), iron in various forms, gold, antimony (tartar emetic), and potassium. Iron is, of course, still used for anaemia, but Robert Darwin used it for stopping bleeding.[27] Another of his favourite chemical remedies was sulphur (or brimstone), that he prescribed mixed with treacle. He often used to say that, 'if people would use it in cases of illness they would have no need to call in medical aid one time in twenty.'[28]

Being a patient in those days was an arduous business. All medicines tasted horrible, and emetics and purges were prescribed for many illnesses. If one avoided these, there were leeches, cupping, blistering and scarification to do battle with. One treatment that was particularly unpleasant was the use of perchloride of iron (it was often known as steel drops) to stop bleeding, both from the nose and from the uterus. In the former case, it could either be injected up the nose, or the nose could be plugged with a sponge soaked in the solution.[29] One of Robert Darwin's patients described what it was like:

> In July I was seized very suddenly with bleeding at the nose to no very common degree. It continued at intervals for ten days, during several of which I was not allowed to be moved, so as even to have my bed eased. Dr Darwin applied the [?drops] of steel, which I do think assisted in subduing the hemmorrhage [sic], but it was most excruciatingly painful, affecting both my eyes and head very intensely.[30]

Alongside herbal and chemical remedies, an important part of the doctor's prescription was advice on food, drink and general lifestyle, then known as a 'regimen'. As we saw in an earlier chapter, one of the key messages in this regard that Robert gave was encouraging his patients to be wise in their consumption of alcohol, a practice that he followed himself.

In the Shropshire Archives there is a prescription from the time of Robert Darwin's, and may even have been written by him.[31] One item prescribed is a liquid (or draught) and the other is a pill. The instructions for taking them are as follows:

> Two of the pills to be taken at night, and two in the forenoon. The draught to be taken with the latter.
> No tea or coffee, but milk and water
> Avoid new bread
> In the morning coffee with a third of a pint of milk and no sugar.

That was typical of the precise dietary advice that was expected by the patient and given by the doctor. Quite how the doctor arrived at the advice is not clear, but Robert had developed a strategy that seemed to work well. Charles wrote:

> When patients who were very ill craved for some strange and unnatural food, my father asked them what had put such an idea into their heads. If they answered that they did not know, he would allow them to try the food, and often with success, as he trusted to their having a kind of instinctive desire. But if they answered that they had heard that the food in question had done good to someone else, he firmly refused his assent.[32]

As well as advising about food and drink, the doctor was often asked for advice about whether the patient needed a change of scene to help their recovery. This was popular with patients and relatives alike, though the rigours of travel meant that the benefits of a change of scene had to be balanced against the effects of the journey. An example of Robert Darwin's advice in this respect is contained in a letter written from Aberystwyth. The lady wrote:

> My old neighbour Miss Pemberton is here – her long attendance on her poor father, together with his loss, has been quite too much for her, and has left her in a very low nervous state. Dr Darwin has ordered her to try the sea, from which I think she seems much recovered.[33]

As we have seen, old Robert Pemberton was a difficult man – doubtless the doctor could see that what his daughter needed was a complete break to grieve and recover physically and emotionally. 'Ordering' her to go to the seaside at the newly fashionable resort of Aberystwyth gave her permission to go away without feeling guilty about leaving the rest of the family.

I wonder how Robert Darwin would have fared under the NHS? I expect he would be delighted that everybody is now treated equally, irrespective of their ability to pay. He might well be relieved that he would not need to be on call twenty-four hours a day, 365 days a year. Doubtless he would find the bureaucracy irksome, as we all do, but probably the biggest difference he would struggle with is the change that has occurred in the doctor-patient relationship in the last 200 years. During Robert's lifetime, an Edinburgh physician, John Brown, published an essay entitled 'The Doctor – Our Duties to Him', in which he listed the four duties that he considered that patients owed their doctors. Brown wrote:

> First, it is your duty to trust the doctor. Secondly, it is your duty to obey the doctor. Thirdly, it is your duty to speak the truth to your doctor, the whole truth, and nothing but the truth; and fourthly, it is your duty to reward the doctor.[34]

Dr Brown illustrated the therapeutic virtue of obedience by telling the story of a man who was given a prescription and told to take it. He returned cured, having eaten the piece of paper on which the prescription was written! An extreme example, of course, but in the days when doctors had so much less to offer than today, it demonstrates the value of the placebo!

Dr Brown mentioned that it was the final duty of the patient to reward the doctor, which naturally leads us to the subject of the next chapter, which is money.

9

THE 'MIDAS TOUCH'

It is interesting to look in more detail at Robert Darwin's financial affairs; they are particularly important in that they played a crucial part in Charles' life. We have already seen that Robert was very astute with money. As he became older his financial affairs became increasingly complex, and he devoted more and more time to them.

To understand this side of Robert's life, it is necessary to provide a very brief background to the supply of money at that time. In a nutshell, it was much more difficult to obtain cash in Georgian England than it is today. Before that time the economy had always depended on land, which provided income through crops, animals and rents. This meant that the small number of people who owned a large proportion of the land had most of the disposable income available, while most of the rest of the population lived a virtually subsistence lifestyle. The number of people in the 'middle classes' (doctors, lawyers, teachers, clergy, and the like) was very small. The change to a money-based economy had been occurring slowly for centuries, but this process accelerated during the Industrial Revolution (approximately 1760-1840). Now the new industrialists needed capital to build their factories, and those who put forward schemes for canals, roads and, later, railways, had to have money up front to pay the construction costs. Also, the gentry wanted to build ever more opulent houses to rival each other, and the increasingly numerous middle classes, which now included prosperous manufacturers and tradesmen, wanted the wherewithal to enable them to own comfortable homes and engage in travel and social activities. In addition, everybody wanted cash in their pockets to pay for the new consumer goods that were increasingly coming onto the market.

So where was all this new money to come from? The government only provided finance for capital schemes if there was a strong defence or political imperative. This happened during the French wars, when some industrialists grew rich on defence contracts. The government also provided the finance for some programmes of civil engineering works, such as those that Thomas Telford masterminded, which included the Holyhead Road that ran past the door of The Mount. For other schemes, banks were a possible source of finance, but in those days they tended to be small, local, and inadequately capitalised, making them liable to collapse. Therefore, for most schemes where money was needed, the only possibility was to seek it from individual investors. Most of the individuals with money were members of the upper classes, but the middle classes, with smaller amounts of surplus cash, were also keen to invest in the new factories and civil engineering works. The drawback for the small investor was that most of these schemes offered only a few large shares, not the large number of small shares that we are accustomed to today. Hence, only the rich could afford to buy shares, unless a number of people clubbed together to share the cost, since there were no stockbrokers outside London in those days. To obtain personal finance for building work or ready money for other purposes, options were limited. Building societies were unknown, as was the Co-operative movement. Mostly people borrowed from relatives or friends if they could, but informal moneylenders were not uncommon. An example of one such is the father of William Hazledine the ironfounder (also William Hazledine), who lent considerable sums of money in small amounts (from £1 to about £40) to many people in the Shawbury area in the late 1700s. He charged around 5 per cent interest.[1]

As we have seen, Robert Darwin quickly became rich, both from money that he and Susannah inherited, and also from his lucrative medical practice. Draft wills for both Robert and Susannah, drawn up in 1808, indicate that at that time they had around £33,000 to invest, of which £13,000 was Robert's and £20,000 Susannah's.[2] This was in addition to the income from the estate near Lincoln left to Robert by his father, and rents from properties they owned adjacent to The Mount. Each year saw a growth in the figure available to invest. For example, the year 1808/9 showed a profit of £2,335.[3] This profit rose steadily year on year, the accounts for 1813/14 showing a profit of £5,500 on a turnover of £9,698, of which around a third was from medical fees.[4]

Robert decided to use this money in a number of ways. First, he gave unsecured loans to both family members and outsiders, coming to an agreement with them on the term of the loan, what interest (if any) he would charge, and how it would be paid back. Secondly, for some large loans he arranged a mortgage, using property or land as security. Thirdly, he bought both government stocks, and shares in canals and roads. Fourthly, he invested money on behalf of others. Finally, he used his financial skill on behalf of the Wedgwood company, advising them and auditing their accounts.[5] In summary, he was a bank, building society, stockbroker and accountant all rolled into one!

Let us look at some of the details of these transactions, beginning with loans to individuals, from which I have picked out a few examples.[6] One person was Charles Bage, who borrowed £334 10s 0d in 1796. Bage was the designer of the Ditherington flax mill in Shrewsbury, the first iron-framed building in the world, which was completed in 1797. The date suggests that this money was used in some way for that project, but as the Benyon brothers financed the actual building of the mill, Bage may have used Robert Darwin's loan to defray the cost of preparing the plans, which he drew up in 1796.[7]

Many other individuals arranged loans with Robert Darwin. For example, Andrew Corbet, a large local landowner, borrowed £400 in 1797; by 1815 Robert Darwin had received £320 15s in interest from this loan, which equates to a rate of 4.5 per cent per annum. John Hiram Haycock, the Darwins' friend and probable designer of their house, borrowed £2,700 over a period of eleven years (1803-14). Presumably this was to enable Haycock to build houses for sale or rent. He paid £408 11s 6d interest, which equates to only around 1.5 per cent per annum over the full term. So either he had a preferential rate of interest, or, perhaps more likely, the borrowing was short term, the money being paid back as each house was sold. In other words, for him Robert's money acted like a bank overdraft. Robert didn't always charge interest on these personal loans. For instance, two ladies called Mrs Cross and Mrs DeCourcy had an interest-free loan in 1811.

The Ditherington flax mill, the first iron-framed building in the world. Robert Darwin lent money to help with its construction. It was later used as a maltings. (Shropshire Archives)

He also lent money to members of his family, even his father, who needed £2,000 in 1800, probably for buying a new house. Erasmus Darwin repaid this loan before his death two years later. The main avenue of family financial support was to his brothers-in-law, Jos and John Wedgwood. Because of the French wars and the fact that neither brother was really interested in running the business, the pottery was struggling. Jos was a reasonable businessman, but John was useless with money, and eventually became insolvent. Robert lent both brothers considerable sums of money, including £30,000 to Jos for the purchase of Maer Hall in 1803.[8] Jos managed to pay him back eventually, but it appears that Robert never did get all his money back from John.[9]

Other investments were more profitable. He continued to gain income from the Lichfield turnpike shares left to him by his grandfather, but most of his investment went into the new canals – The Grand Trunk, Shropshire, Shrewsbury and Ellesmere. Some of the shares he put in trusts for the children, and these provided good earnings from dividends. For example, he was able to credit Marianne and Caroline with £60 each in 1814. Perhaps because it was wartime, Robert didn't invest much in government stocks, but did buy some 4 per cent annuities, probably on behalf of Jos Wedgwood. He also invested in 6 per cent American stocks, which made a loss, but Robert consoled himself with the fact that 'the loss was less than if I had invested in English stocks.'[10]

As well as investing his own money, he also acted on behalf of small investors, about twenty of whom are listed in his account books. Presumably Robert got to know them as patients, so they trusted him with their money A good number of them were women – Robert Darwin's help would have been especially invaluable for unmarried women and widows, whose income often derived from the interest from investments. Robert explained what he did in the case of Miss Martha Congreve, writing that in 1796 he 'paid her the interest allowed on £25 in her share in the Ellesmere Canal standing in my name.'[11]

Pontcysyllte Aqueduct on the Llangollen Canal around 1830, by the artist Isaac Shaw. Robert Darwin helped to finance the construction of the canal. (Shrewsbury Museums Service)

The first record the author can find of Robert providing a loan using property as security is in 1807. These were called mortgages, though technically they were re-mortgages, since the property was already in the possession of the person requesting the loan. On this occasion he lent a total of £20,000 to William Lacon Childe and his associates, some of whose lands in the far south of Shropshire around Cleobury Mortimer were security for the deal.[12]

He also had a lot of dealings with the Mytton family, who owned large estates in what was then Montgomeryshire, now Powys. Richard Mytton (1751-1828) inherited the estate from his grandfather in 1809 and wished to embark on an ambitious and extravagant development of his main house at Garth, near Guilsfield.[13, 14] For this, of course, he needed money, and plenty of it, so he turned to Robert Darwin, who obliged with a loan of around £20,000, secured on a mortgage of part of the estate.[15] Richard Mytton's later career involved going back to Cambridge from 1818 to 1821, during which time he was ordained. In February 1827 he became chaplain to the Governor General of India, whence he sailed with his young wife and two children. For some reason they set off to return home the following year, but Mytton died on the return voyage. His neighbour, Viscount Clive, later the Earl of Powys, then administered Mytton's affairs on behalf of Charlotte, Mytton's widow. The first thing they needed to do was to pay off some of Mytton's debts, so they attempted to sell the Trefnanney estate.[16] Perhaps due to the unfavourable economic climate the sale was not successful, so once again they turned to Robert Darwin for help. On this occasion he lent them £25,000 in two parts – £5,000 in January, and £20,000 in April 1829, the loan to last for 1,000 years![17] The interest from

Garth Hall near Welshpool, 1940, just before its demolition. Robert Darwin lent £20,000 for its construction. (Royal Commission on the Ancient and Historical Monuments of Wales)

1829-1834 was 4.5 per cent per annum, which means that Robert was paid £562 10s per half year.[18] From 1834 the interest rate dropped to 4 per cent, which meant a drop of income for Robert to £500 a half year. This continued until 1843, when the introduction of property tax of 3 per cent on the interest earned reduced the half yearly payments to £484 3s 7d.[19] By my reckoning, the interest that Robert Darwin received in the years 1829-43 was around £16,396. Among other things, Robert used this income to finance Charles' five-year *Beagle* voyage, which took place during these years.

What motivated Robert Darwin to spend so much time and effort making all this money? Historians tend to describe him as 'ruthless' when it came to making money,[20] and that opinion was shared by at least some of his contemporaries. This view is encapsulated by a story that was still circulating fifty years after his death. The writer recalled:

> Dr Darwin was a sharp man of business, and always kept his eye on the 'needful'. He was once sent for in a great hurry to see a patient who lived a few miles away in the country. The gentleman was a member of a firm of bankers in Shrewsbury, at whose bank the doctor had deposited a large sum of money. When he arrived at the house he found the gentleman had just committed suicide, and was consequently beyond the doctor's power to aid. Refreshments had been provided, but he hurriedly departed, stepped into his carriage, and when he had gained the high road, gave the coachman orders to drive as fast as possible back to Shrewsbury and straight to the bank, where he arrived before the news of the sad affair had reached the town.

> On entering the bank he requested that a sum of money which was lying there may be given him, which was done, when he told the manager what had occurred. The next day the bank suspended payment, closed its doors, and finally failed.[21]

This story was well known to Charles, whose version is totally different. This is what he wrote:

> I remember a story, showing how easily utterly false beliefs originate and spread. Mr E[yton], a squire of one of the oldest families in Shropshire, and head partner in a bank, committed suicide. My father was sent for as a matter of form, and found him dead … My father, in returning home, thought it proper to call at the bank (where he had an account) to tell the managing partner of the event, as it was not improbable it would cause a run on the bank. Well, the story was spread far and wide that my father went into the bank, drew out all his money, left the bank, came back again, and said, 'I may tell you that Mr E has killed himself', and then departed. It seems that it was then a common belief that money withdrawn from a bank was not safe until the person had passed out through the door of the bank. My father did not hear this story till some little time afterwards, when the managing partner said that he had departed from his invariable rule of never allowing any one to see the account of another man, by having shown the ledger with my father's account to several persons, as this proved that my father had not drawn out a penny on that day. It would have been dishonourable in my father to have used his professional knowledge for his private advantage.[22]

Personally I prefer Charles' version – it feels more true to the Robert Darwin I have found. He was certainly a financial wheeler-dealer, perhaps verging on ruthlessness at times, but he would have considered it beneath himself to be dishonest. He was often generous with his money, giving interest-free loans to some and gifts to the poor, and he also often gave to charity, the recorded examples of which are presumably representative of much more.[23]

He used his money to live very comfortably, but he was not ostentatious, unlike many of his rich contemporaries. So what drove him to make so much money? I think the answer may lie chiefly in his early experiences. His father, who was never good with money, found that his second marriage stretched his finances to the limit, since his new wife liked good living, and their many children needed to be supported. The result was that Robert was forced into a profession he hated, at least initially, and was largely left by his father to sink or swim. Robert may well have determined that the same would never happen to his children. During much of his life, five of the six children were financially dependent on him, which would have made the burden of provision for them all the more acute.

It may also have been that, especially later in life when the need to make money was much less, he just enjoyed doing so. Perhaps the pleasure was increased by the fact that he, the outsider, the unbeliever and political liberal, made much of his money from lending to the nobility – Anglicans and Tories to a man. Who knows?

However, we are getting ahead of ourselves. We need to back-track a little to look at what happened to the Darwins in the two decades after Charles left for Edinburgh.

10

A TIME OF CHANGE

In October 1825 Charles and Eras Darwin set off together on the long journey north to study medicine at Edinburgh University. In this they were following in the footsteps of their grandfather Erasmus, father Robert, and their ill-fated Uncle Charles. Eras had already been studying in Cambridge for three years. Robert took advantage of his elder son's move to Edinburgh for the clinical part of the course as an ideal way of releasing Charles from his unhappy time at Shrewsbury School. The plan was that the older boy would look after his brother, who, though young, was the same age as Robert had been when he went away to university. Robert was full of optimism about the move. He was nearly sixty, and longed to have his sons join him in his medical practice, first to ease the interminable workload, and then in time to take over the practice completely.

Perhaps Robert's optimism was tempered by anxiety. He remembered only too vividly that he had felt trapped by his father's plans as he himself embarked on his medical education over forty years earlier. He did not wish his sons to suffer a similar fate, and he probably sensed that Eras was already unhappy about the idea of becoming a doctor. He therefore especially encouraged Charles' interest in medicine by arranging for him to look after some of his patients during the summer before he went away. As a result of this experience Robert was able to pronounce that Charles 'would make a successful physician,'[1] perhaps recognising the strength of Charles' sympathetic personality as he related to patients.

Robert hardly ever wrote personal letters, a practice he acknowledged in a letter to Charles much later, saying, 'You know I never write anything besides answering questions about medicine … '[2], so he relied on the regular flow of letters from his daughters to keep in touch with his sons, but the lack of letters did not mean that Robert was not interested in them. Far from it, for he passed on many messages of advice, encouragement and love. For example, Susan wrote, 'Papa says Erasmus may wear flannel next to his skin in cold weather by all means, and that he may sleep in it also, tho' he does not think that very adviseable [sic] – but in warm weather he very much objects to it.'[3] And in a later letter, 'Papa says you are a very good lad for remembering to mention Johnson [a fellow student from Shrewsbury] … Papa desires his love to the Boy Tactus and the man Daggy [presumably Robert's pet names for his sons].'[4]

But things did not go as the father hoped. Eras only stayed in Edinburgh a year, and though he qualified, he never practised medicine, apart from looking after a few of his father's patients in the spring of 1826.[5] In Edinburgh Charles found most of the lectures unbelievably dull. Like his father he hated the sight of blood, and he found operations done without anaesthetic so horrific that he ran out, never to darken the doors again. Word reached Shrewsbury that Charles was picking and choosing which lectures to attend, which increased Robert's anxiety, and he swiftly sent a message via Susan urging his son to reconsider.[6] This had a temporary effect[7], but Charles could not wait for the session to finish so he could get back home to enjoy the shooting and fishing.[8]

As far as possible Charles stayed away from his father during that summer, trying to avoid discussions about his lack of application. He returned to Edinburgh alone for the next academic year, but it soon became obvious that he had no real intention of practising as a doctor. Robert wisely did not force him to continue, as his own father had done with him, and proposed instead that Charles transfer to Cambridge to study to become a clergyman. To us this may seem a strange suggestion, considering that Robert was an unbeliever, but he probably already realised that Charles was interested in natural history, and that if he was going to pursue this interest the best way would be to become a clergyman. In those days there were almost no professional scientists, and most people who studied natural history were clergymen with independent means. These men often had an undemanding country parish that gave plenty of time for study and reflection. Probably the plan was that Robert, with his many influential connections, would have found his son a suitable living so that he could pursue his interest in natural history. With these plans in mind Charles went up to Cambridge in the autumn of 1828, where he stayed until 1831.

The period after Charles left home seems to have been quite a dark time for Robert. His health was not very good, and he had to come to terms with the fact that neither of his sons was going to follow in his footsteps. As compensation he seems to have worked increasingly with his son-in-law Henry Parker.[9] Caroline was twenty-five, Susan was twenty-two, and Catherine was fifteen when Charles left for Edinburgh, and Robert must have felt that The Mount was filled with young women and their friends. Much as he loved them, Robert longed for the companionship of Susannah, whose loss he still felt deeply. He tended to react to the presence of all these young people by becoming increasingly irritable and overbearing, insisting on dominating the conversation when at last he reached home after a long day's work. Elizabeth Wedgwood, one of the girls' cousins from Maer Hall, wrote of one Sunday when she visited. 'We dined at half past one, drest [sic] afterwards, and sat about three hours expecting the tide to come in [i.e. Robert's return home] about dark, and rather stiff and formal the evening was.'[10] Emma Wedgwood, Charles' future wife, writing perhaps when she stayed during New Year 1826,[11] said that 'she was extremely glad when the Dr went off on a long journey, and sorry to see him come back again.'[12] One must remember, however, that these correspondents were just teenagers (Emma was fifteen at the time) who were used to doing much as they pleased, and so tended to resent any restriction on their freedom. Another niece gave a more positive view of her uncle. She wrote, 'My uncle, Dr Robert Darwin, was a tall, very large man, weighing more than 20 stone, but wonderfully active for his size and very fond of his garden. He was extremely cheerful and agreeable, full of amusing anecdotes, and considered a very clever doctor.'[13]

The language and contents of the letters that the sisters wrote to Charles give little support to the view that Robert was a 'tyrant', and the atmosphere at The Mount uniformly gloomy and foreboding, as one writer has maintained.[14] On the contrary, many visitors stayed at the house, which was often also the setting for entertaining, when the girls, especially Susan and Catherine, liked nothing better than doing a bit of flirting. The girls often went for walks and

Mount House from the north, date and artist unknown. (Transactions of the Shropshire Archaeological and Natural History Society, 1884)

rides in the country, and spent much time visiting family and friends. On one occasion a friend told Charles that, 'I think Caroline and Catherine will have a very pleasant junket to the Isle of Wight. Have you heard that Susan positively declines leaving "sweet 'ome", though Erasmus offered to take her to Paris, or any part of the Continent?'[15] Hardly the reaction of a young woman who hated being at home!

In the season the girls enjoyed the social round that culminated in the hunt ball. On winter evenings they and their father would often read together from a book borrowed from the newly opened lending library, or listen to Caroline or Susan playing the piano. Their lives may have appeared a bit dull at times, but there was much to do with organising the house and gardens, being receptionist and secretary for their father, and running the infant school.

But it was all too dull for Eras, who had experienced the delights of the intellectual life of Cambridge, and had no desire to return to sleepy Shrewsbury. He therefore moved to London. Robert clearly acquiesced in this decision, since Eras never worked, and relied for his income entirely on his father's generosity.

Eras' closest friend in London was his cousin Hensleigh Wedgwood, youngest son of Josiah Wedgwood II, and hence brother of Charles's future wife Emma. Hensleigh and Eras became part of a literary and artistic circle that included Thomas and Jane Carlyle, John Ruskin, George Eliot, Elizabeth Gaskell, Harriet Martineau and Henry Wadsworth Longfellow, among others. During this time Hensleigh was courting Fanny Mackintosh, the daughter of Sir James Mackintosh, politician and historian. Mackintosh had married Hensleigh's mother's sister, so he and Fanny were cousins. After they married in 1832, Fanny was always known as 'Fanny Hensleigh' to distinguish her from various other Fannies in the family! It was not long before Eras seemed to be visiting the Hensleigh Wedgwoods more often than just his friendship with Hensleigh required.

While all this was going on Charles was also taking advantage of his father's generosity, doing as little work as he could on his course at Cambridge. He ran up many bills, which his father

Professor J.S. Henslow in 1849, by T.H. Maguire.

– 'the Governor', as Charles called him – had to foot. A typical example was one for £200 (around £8,000 at today's prices),[16] but at least he was developing his natural history education, especially through his friendship with Professor John Stevens Henslow. Henslow was a fount of knowledge not only on botany, his principle subject, but also entomology, chemistry, mineralogy and geology. Henslow was also a clergyman of orthodox views, 'whose moral qualities were in every way admirable'.[17] It was through Henslow that Charles was offered the post as naturalist on the *Beagle*.

The problem was that this post was unpaid – in fact, the successful applicant had to pay £500 up front, £30 a year thereafter, and also meet all his own expenses on the voyage.[18] And so it was time to apply to 'the Governor' again, as Charles had no hope of going unless his father paid. Robert was exasperated with his son's request. For the past five years he had given Charles all he wanted, with little evidence that his son had any intention of becoming anything but 'an idle sporting man.'[19] Robert had supported him in one change of career, and now he was suggesting something else, for which he had no training or experience. The father was also anxious for his son's safety, knowing full well the dangers from weather, native tribes and disease that such a voyage could bring. Above all, he wanted the best for his son, and he 'thought the voyage hazardous to his happiness,' as he wrote to Henslow later.[20] For all these reasons, Robert objected strongly to the proposal, but added the words that Charles remembered so well, 'If you can find any man of common sense, who advises you to go, I will give my consent.'[21]

Although Charles wrote to Henslow to say he could not go on the *Beagle*, he had by no means given up the idea. He wrote in his autobiography that the day after declining the *Beagle* offer, 'I went to Maer [his Uncle Jos' estate] to be ready for September 1st [the start of the shooting season], and whilst out shooting my uncle sent for me, offering to drive me over to Shrewsbury and talk with my father.'[22] The impression given by these words, which has persisted to this day, is that Robert was unreasonable, and it required great courage and persistence on Charles' part, and the support of his uncle, to make his father change his mind. The reality seems rather different, for on 30 August Robert himself took the initiative, writing the following to his brother-in-law:

Maer Hall, home of Josiah Wedgwood II and his family. (Originally published in Wedgwood, Barbara and Hensleigh, *The Wedgwood Circle* Studio Vista, 1980 – reproduced courtesy of Sir Martin Wedgwood)

> Charles will tell you of the offer he has had made to him of going for a voyage of discovery for 2 years. I strongly object to it on various grounds, but I will not detail my reasons that he may have your unbiassed [sic] opinion on the subject, and if you think differently from me I shall wish him to follow your advice.[23]

Charles must have taken this letter with him the next day to Maer and discussed the contents with his uncle, and also the rest of the Wedgwood family, for he wrote to his father on 31 August:

> I am afraid I am going to make you again very uncomfortable. But upon consideration, I think you will excuse me once again stating my opinions on the offer of the voyage. My excuse and reason is the different way all the Wedgwoods view the subject from what you and my sisters do.
>
> I have given Uncle Jos what I fervently trust is an accurate and full list of your objections, and he is kind enough to give his opinion on all. The list and his answers will be enclosed. But may I beg of you one favor [sic], it will be doing me the greatest kindness if you will send me a decided answer, yes or no. If the latter, I should be most ungrateful if I did not implicitly yield to your better judgment and to the kindest indulgence which you have shown me all through my life. And you may rely upon it that I will never mention the subject again. If your answer should be yes, I will go directly to Henslow and consult deliberately with him, and then come to Shrewsbury. The danger appears to me and all the Wedgwoods not great. The expence [sic] can not be serious, and the time I do not think anyhow would be more thrown away than if I staid [sic] at home. But pray do not consider that I am bent on going, that I would for one *single moment* [his italics] hesitate, if you thought, that after a short period, you should continue uncomfortable.
>
> I must again state I cannot think it would unfit me hereafter for a steady life. I do hope this letter will not give you much uneasiness. I send it by the car tomorrow morning. If you make up your mind directly will you send me an answer on the following day, by the same means. If this letter should not find you at home, I hope you will answer as soon as you conveniently can.

> I do not know what to say about Uncle Jos' kindness, I never can forget how he interests himself about me.
>
> Believe me my dear Father,
> Yours affectionate son,
> Charles Darwin[24]

I have quoted the whole letter because the tone seems to me rather like emotional blackmail, comparing the apparently 'unreasonable' Darwins to the 'reasonable' Wedgwoods, and using a combination of fawning and flattery to obtain the desired end. Be that as it may, it had the desired effect, for Robert Darwin wrote back to Josiah Wedgwood the following day:

> Charles is very grateful for your taking so much trouble and interest in his plans. I made up my mind to give up all objections, if you should not see it in the same view as I did.
>
> Charles has stated my objections quite fairly and fully – if he still continues in the same mind after further enquiry, I will give him all the assistance in my power.
>
> Many thanks for your kindness,
> Yours affectionately,
> RW Darwin[25]

Presumably the letter had already gone when Charles and his uncle arrived at The Mount after their ride over from Maer. Rather than the lengthy debate that is implied in Charles' version of the story, there was a warm reception – the father's decision was already made.

This very important incident in Charles' life rather begs the question, 'How much can we rely on his autobiography?' The autobiography has been trawled through for generations, and has been the subject of much criticism. Stephen Jay Gould, a well-known Darwinian scientist, has even called it 'maddeningly misleading'.[26] Darwin's most recent major biographer agrees with this assessment when she calls the autobiography 'a smokescreen'[27], and 'a camouflage … a disguise'.[28]

The explanation of the vagueness and discrepancies between what Charles wrote and what actually happened could well be that the autobiography was written over forty years after many of the events, and, because it was not intended for publication, that Charles did not check the facts carefully. Probably he did not intend to deceive, but his inconsistency or vagueness sometimes makes one wonder if he is not trying, at the very least, to put the best possible 'spin' on events. This appears to be the case with the details of what happened before he went on the *Beagle* voyage. I hope that by carefully re-examining the original letters, Robert Darwin has been rescued from the oft-repeated image of being an unreasonable obstacle in his son's route to greatness.

Robert's generosity allowed his son to go on the life-changing voyage, but he was no pushover. As Robert, Uncle Jos and Charles talked about the costs of the expedition, Charles, trying again to butter his father up, said that, 'I should be deuced clever to spend more than my allowance whilst on board the *Beagle*'. But his father, who understood his son's character better than he seems to have done himself, answered with a smile, 'But they all tell me you are very clever.'[29]

11

A MOMENTOUS DECADE

After weeks of delay due to unfavourable winds, HMS *Beagle*, with Charles Darwin on board, eventually managed to leave English waters on 27 December 1831. Beagle finally returned to Falmouth on 2 October 1836, the voyage, which was intended to last two years, in the end stretched to nearly five. Back in Shrewsbury, the three unmarried sisters, Caroline (thirty-one), Susan (twenty-eight) and Catherine (twenty-one), decided on a plan for keeping in touch. Taking it in turn, each girl would write once every three months, so that hopefully Charles would get a letter each month written by a different sister. They agreed that they would only mention things that had already happened, otherwise Charles would become confused wondering whether things mentioned were past or present. In this way he would be able to build up a log of all that was happening in Shrewsbury.[1] Generally the plan worked well, and Charles expressed his appreciation, writing nearly two years into the voyage that, 'I now thank you all … for writing so very regularly – no one in the *Beagle* has received so uniform a series of letters. I shall return to Shropshire quite au fait with the latest news.'[2] He was enjoying his adventure, but he knew that 'no one ever had a better or dearer lot to say farewell to.'[3]

During the five years he was away, the Shrewsbury family suffered a rollercoaster of emotions. There was a continued anxiety about Charles' safety, and each letter from him was eagerly anticipated. Once the letter was received, the anxiety was dissipated for a while, only to build up again as the weeks passed with no news. Of course they did not like to express these anxieties to Charles, but time and again the relief they felt can be gauged from the letters. For example, Susan wrote, 'On the 3rd of May we received your last letter written from St Salvador, which all the house rejoiced over most heartily … '[4] Even his father Robert, who never wrote social letters, wrote once or twice, saying on one occasion, with obvious understatement, 'We all are very happy when we get a letter from you.'[5]

Charles' letters home were often sent on to other members of the family, such as Eras or the Parkers, and family friends. They, in turn, shared their letters. Charles became quite a celebrity with his young Parker nephews, who followed his voyages on the map. Susan told him, 'Master Parky [Robert, then aged seven] went through the whole of your voyage as a geographical lesson, so Marianne [his mother] made profit as well as pleasure from your letter.'[6] Gradually the Shrewsbury family realised that Charles was becoming quite a celebrity with people who

HMS *Beagle* in the Strait of Magellan. (Originally published in an 1890 version of Charles Darwin's *Journal of Researches into the Geology and Natural History of Various Countries Visited by HMS* Beagle)

mattered, such as Professors Henslow and Sedgwick at Cambridge. Susan shared their pleasure with her brother in a letter:

> Dr Butler [of Shrewsbury School] sent Papa an extract from a letter of Professor Sedgwick's to him which was as follows about you. 'He is doing admirably in S. America, and has already sent home a collection above all praise. It was the best thing in the world for him that he went out on the voyage of discovery. There was some risk of his turning out an idle man, but his character will now be fixed, and if God spare his life, he will have a great name among the naturalists of Europe.'[7]

They came to understand that Charles' first love in the future was to be science. This is evidenced when he wrote, 'Give my best love to Marianne. We do not write to each other for the same reason, we are too busy with our children. She with Master Robert & Henry etc, I with Master Megatherium and Mastodon [fossils].'[8] As well as personal letters, Charles also sent them a copy of his journal, which they read aloud together on winter evenings.[9] Caroline wrote that his style left something to be desired, but encouraged him to 'remember, this criticism only applies to parts of your journal, the greatest part I like exceedingly, and could find no fault, and all of it I had the greatest pleasure in reading.'[10] Susan was not backward in pointing out errors of spelling or grammar, but she did say that, 'I daresay these errors are the effect of haste, but as your Granny it is my duty to point them out.'[11]

These letters help us to understand a little better the characters of the sisters. Susan often signed herself 'Granny', a nickname that she cheerfully applied to herself, for she knew that she tended to be bossy. She comes over as a practical person, a good organiser, not backward in expressing her opinion, and sometimes a bit waspish, especially when it came to news of Eras.

Caroline, however, seems much more motherly, a 'people person' who longed for the best for her former charge. Charles called her 'my Governess' – the nearest thing he had to a mother.[12] Catherine's character is more difficult to gauge from her letters, but she seems to have been more of a gossip and socialite, perhaps envious of Charles' freedom and impatient to have him back in the family fold.

For the three sisters, life in Shrewsbury carried on in a similar vein to that before Charles left. Caroline was busy with the school, which she reorganised into the new building in the autumn of 1833.[13] Then there were their father's patients to look after and the household to run, though doubtless the large and experienced staff of servants did most of the work. So there was plenty of time for leisure, with many trips to relatives and friends, including a memorable one for Susan and Catherine to London in May 1833. They also had many visitors who stayed at The Mount.

One of the unsolved mysteries surrounding the four Darwin sisters is that we have no definite portraits of any of them. The miniature that was for many years thought to be of Caroline[14] is now considered to be of her aunt, Jane Wedgwood (née Allen).[15] It is highly likely that the girls did have their pictures painted, for on 18 May 1830 Richard Thomas Lloyd described in a letter how he was 'sitting for his portrait by Miss Owen at Dr Darwin's'.[16] The artist, one of the Owens of Woodhouse, may well have painted the Darwin girls as well, either at this or another time. The Shrewsbury Museum has a picture entitled 'Portrait of a Young Woman (possibly a Darwin or Wedgwood)'. The artist is thought to be George Richmond; the precise date is unknown, but it may be 1842. The sitter looks to me no older than in her early thirties, and seems to bear a resemblance to the likeness of Robert Darwin. If this is indeed one of the Darwin sisters, and the date is in early 1840s, the obvious candidate would be Catherine, who was then around thirty.

And what did Robert feel about Charles while he was away? He may not have written many letters, but he made his love and commitment to his son abundantly clear in messages sent in his daughters' letters. At the risk of repetition, here are some examples:

> 'Papa bids me tell you with his love … '[17]
>
> 'Papa desires I will give you his most affectionate love, and many thanks for your very nice letter which has given him a great deal of pleasure.'[18]
>
> 'Papa sends his most affectionate love to you, and bids me again repeat what we have all said continually. [Which is] how much we hope we may depend upon your not allowing any false shame to prevent your returning whenever you feel inclined. It would make us all so happy to have you back again.'[19]
>
> 'Papa desires his most affectionate love to you. We all often talk about you and you are forgotten by nobody, I assure you … '[20]
>
> 'My dear Charles, ever your affectionate, RW Darwin.'[21]
>
> 'Papa particularly enjoyed your last letter, and desires me to tell you most affectionately from him that he is *exceedingly* [her italics] glad you have engaged a servant, as he is sure it will conduce very much to your comfort, and only regrets you had not one sooner … Papa and all send their very best loves to you … '[22]
>
> 'Papa, who never forgets anniversarys [sic], remembered this day of course at breakfast, and sends you his best love and blessing on reaching 25 years.'[23]
>
> 'Papa is very well and very anxious to have further news of you. All here send their affectionate love to you.'[24]
>
> 'We are now reading it [his journal] aloud, and Papa enjoys it extremely, except when the dangers

Portrait, which may be of Catherine Darwin, by George Richmond, *c.* 1842. (Shrewsbury Museums Service)

you run make him shudder ...'[25]

From these quotes we can feel the affection the father felt for his son. We see Robert delighted at his son's success, but keen to reassure him that it would be no shame if he wanted to come home early. Robert was also more than happy to bear the cost of employing a servant to ensure that Charles was comfortable. The father also shuddered with a mixture of pride and anxiety at the risks his son was exposed to on the voyage. In his turn Charles was bowled over by the

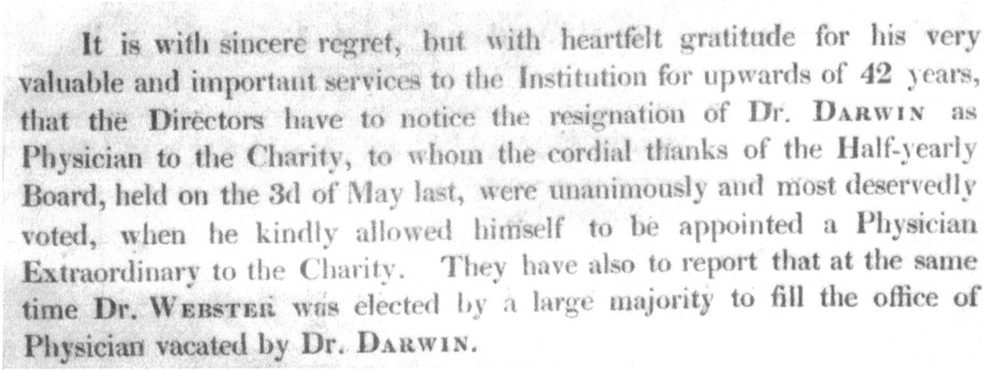

It is with sincere regret, but with heartfelt gratitude for his very valuable and important services to the Institution for upwards of 42 years, that the Directors have to notice the resignation of Dr. DARWIN as Physician to the Charity, to whom the cordial thanks of the Half-yearly Board, held on the 3d of May last, were unanimously and most deservedly voted, when he kindly allowed himself to be appointed a Physician Extraordinary to the Charity. They have also to report that at the same time Dr. WEBSTER was elected by a large majority to fill the office of Physician vacated by Dr. DARWIN.

A minute regarding Dr Darwin's retirement from the Salop Infirmary. (Shropshire Archives)

evidence of his father's love. For example, he wrote, 'I have just received a bundle more letters. I do not know how to thank you all sufficiently – one from Catherine … another from Susan … together with notes from Caroline and from my father. I almost cried for pleasure at receiving it. It was very kind, thinking of writing to me … '[26]

Charles' evident success was one factor helping to make Robert far more contented than he had ever been since Susannah's death. Another reason was the gradual slowing down of his medical practice. We have noted that in 1831 he resigned his post as physician to the Salop Infirmary. The following note in the Infirmary Minutes marked the occasion:

> It is with sincere regret, but with heartfelt gratitude for his very valuable and important services to the Institution for upwards of 42 years, that the Directors have to notice the resignation of Dr Darwin as physician to the Charity, to whom the cordial thanks of the Half-yearly Board, held on May 31st last, were unanimously and most deservedly voted, when he kindly allowed himself to be appointed a Physician Extraordinary to the Charity.[27]

A 'Physician Extraordinary' was like an Emeritus Professor, a title given to those who had retired after meritorious service. The position allowed the holder to advise and be consulted if necessary, especially if the physicians and surgeons could not agree on the wisdom of treatments such as amputation. Despite being freed from the burden of the infirmary work, it took a good deal of persuasion from the daughters to encourage Robert to really slow down. Susan wrote in August 1832, 'Papa has not been as well as usual lately, he has had the lumbago and altogether finds the least exertion too much for him. We are persuading him as much as possible to give up going out to see patients, and then he would avoid any hurry or fatigue.'[28]

It seems that the sisters' persuasion bore fruit, for we find Susan writing to Charles soon after, 'You will be surprised to hear that my father has at last put his long talked of scheme into execution and set out to London two days ago with Caroline inside, and Edward and Harry the brother antiquarians on the seat behind, as upon our Lincolnshire tour.'[29] (The reference to the 'brother antiquarians' is a joke about the old servants Edward, the butler, and Harry.) This trip was obviously very successful, since Susan adds later in the letter, 'We have heard twice from London, and they bring very agreeable accounts of my father. He does not seem so much tired by sight seeing as Caroline expected, and enjoys it all excessively. The Zoological Garden he had been to once … '[30]

Robert enjoyed it so much that he soon went on another tour. Susan wrote from London:

> We left dear Papa very well, and in very good spirits. He is become so spirited in touring, that he and Caroline went very lately on another very beautiful tour in Yorkshire. They went by Liverpool, which Papa had never seen, saw the Rail Road, but did not go on it. Then went on to the beautiful Yorkshire Abbeys, and so on to York Cathedral, and home by Litchfield [sic]. They were absent about ten days, and the tour answered most perfectly to Papa, who enjoyed it most exceedingly and came back in much better health than he started.[31]

Later that year it was Susan rather than Caroline who accompanied her father to see the Cathedrals of Gloucester, Winchester and Salisbury, which Robert again enjoyed greatly.[32, 33] The last trip recorded in the letters was one that Robert and Caroline took to Wales, enjoying the warm May weather of 1834.[34]

As well as touring, Robert found a new interest in the recently built hot house, which was finished about the time Charles started his *Beagle* voyage. Susan wrote to him that, 'Our hot house is quite finished, and we have got several Pines [pineapples] and plants in it. Papa sits there a great deal and it answers very well as a hobby for him. We have had pipes laid in the greenhouse [the conservatory attached to the morning room] and the regular warmth of the hot water makes the morning room very comfortable as it was apt to get very cold at night.'[35] Charles wrote back, encouraging them to grow a banana tree, which they did. Robert wrote to his son, 'In consequence of the recommendation in your first letter I got a banana tree. It flourishes so as to promise to fill the hothouse. I sit under it, and think of you in similar shade.'[36]

However, Robert's contentment was clouded by rumours coming from London about Erasmus. His sisters, though they always liked their good-natured brother, found him thoroughly frustrating. Susan wrote to Charles, 'You really must not blame me if Eras does not write to you, for I regularly send him a dun [an old word for 'to plague or pester'] in every postscript [of her letters to him] … If he comes down at Easter I will stand over him and torment his heart out about writing to you.'[37] Although always retiring by nature, and a man who preferred talk to action, it is possible that Erasmus' indolence was more than just his nature. Charles wrote to Caroline after his return, '[I] see scarcely anything of Erasmus, but he appeared very well and in good spirits the day he dined with us. He takes no wine or smoke, but sticks to his opium with many groans.'[38] Was Erasmus, then, an opium addict? The fact that he appeared to be taking opium, even though otherwise well, and the talk of 'groans', which could suggest opiate withdrawal, makes one wonder. Addiction to opium would certainly help to explain his chronic lethargy.

Always a lady's man, who happily escorted married women around in his fashionable cab, the talk now was of Erasmus' infatuation with his cousin Hensleigh's wife, Fanny. Susan wrote to Charles in August 1832, 'Mr and Mrs Hensleigh [i.e. Hensleigh and Fanny] are at Maer, and coming to see us early in September, and I expect that by *some chance* [her emphasis] Erasmus will then appear among us, for there is certainly great attraction in that quarter.[39] Perhaps one of Robert's incentives to go to London was to talk to his son about the matter, but if so it seems not to have been very successful, for the following year Catherine wrote to Charles from London:

> We see a great deal of Erasmus now, as our lodgings are not very far from his, and he is good-natured and pleasant, we enjoy it very much. Driving in his cab is one of the pleasantest things possible, and he drives so very well I am not afraid, even in a London crowd. He seems to be more in love than ever with Fanny Hensleigh, and almost lives at Clapham [the Hensleigh Wedgwood's home].

> Papa has long been *alarmed* for consequences, and expects to see an *action* [both her emphases] in the papers. I think the real danger is with Miss Emma Wedgwood, who I suspect Mr Erasmus to be more in love with than appears, or than perhaps he knows himself.[40]

In the event, Eras' indolence, coupled with Hensleigh's apparent blindness to what was going on, avoided an open scandal. Erasmus and Fanny remained very close, but there is no evidence to suppose that there was anything more than a deep friendship between them. Eras also found fulfilment in becoming a surrogate uncle/father figure to her children, especially the younger daughters Hope and Effie.[41] As for Emma Wedgwood, that naturally brings us on to Robert Darwin's next reason for happiness.

As Charles' long-awaited return drew closer, the family naturally wondered what he would do next. Susan wrote to him on his birthday in February 1836, 'Papa and we often cogitate over the fire what you will do when you return, as I fear there are but small hopes of you still going into the Church. I think you must turn Professor at Cambridge and marry a Miss Jenner if there is one to be had.'[42] (The reference to 'Miss Jenner' is a presumably a joke that as a great scientist he would need to marry the daughter of a similarly great scientist like Edward Jenner.) In the end Charles' return took his family by surprise, and he walked into The Mount early on Wednesday 5 October 1836.

His life had been turned upside down, and soon another of the residents of The Mount would also have a complete change. It had been nearly fifteen years since Bessy Wedgwood had written that Caroline Darwin would make a wonderful wife for her son Josiah III (usually known as Joe). Whether anything had been said in the meantime between the two families is not recorded, but suddenly in May 1837, Joe, then forty-two, asked Caroline to marry him. During the intervening years he had reluctantly joined the pottery, plodding steadily towards making enough money to escape. Perhaps he felt that by 1837 his time for release had come, or that, if he left it any longer, he and Caroline would miss the chance of having children. The characters of the two are summed up in a letter that Charles wrote to his cousin William Darwin Fox just after the engagement was announced:

> Caroline is going to be married to Jos [Joe] Wedgwood … He is a very quiet grave man, with very much to like and respect in him, but I wish he would put himself forward more. He has a most wonderful deal of information and is a very superior person, but he has not made the most of himself. I am very glad of the marriage for Caroline's sake, as I think she will be a very happy person, especially if she has children, for I never saw a human being so fond of little crying wretches, as she is.[43]

Joe's mother was overjoyed, commenting that she was as 'pleased as if Joe had won Victoria herself', a reference to their new sovereign.[44] Joe even hinted that he was not as unemotional a man as everyone thought, writing to his uncle (and now prospective father-in-law) to thank him for his daughter's hand:

> … Thanking you in the warmest manner for your kind expressions towards me, I am beyond measure delighted with my good fortune in obtaining a woman whose disposition, understanding and amiable and agreeable qualities I so much admire. On no account are you to show this letter to her. Having indulged in as much rapture as a man of 42 can venture on I shall be more sober for the future and not exhibit such a common want of self command as I have done.[45]

St George's Church, *c.* 1850. (Henry Pidgeon, *Memorials of Shrewsbury* J.H. Leake, Shrewsbury, 1850)

Joe and Caroline were married on 4 August 1837 – theirs was the fourth wedding at the new St George's Church, Frankwell, just down the road from The Mount. Caroline was aged thirty-seven, and was five years younger than her bridegroom; at the signing of the register Erasmus and Robert Darwin were the witnesses.[46] The newly-weds moved to a house near Maer in Staffordshire, where Joe continued in the pottery firm for the time being. They had a good financial start to their marriage – Joe's father, Jos, contributed a bond of £5,000, which produced an income of £400 a year, while Robert Darwin gave £10,000.[47, 48] Charles' wish that his sister would have children was soon granted, for a daughter, Sophy, was born the following year.

Josiah Wedgwood III. (Originally published in Wedgwood, Barbara and Hensleigh, *The Wedgwood Circle* Studio Vista, 1980 – reproduced courtesy of Sir Martin Wedgwood)

It was soon Caroline's turn to be happy for her brother Charles, for in November 1838 Charles announced his engagement to Emma Wedgwood. Caroline wrote as soon as she heard:

> I must this very evening give you joy of having secured the very sweetest, most sympathetic of wives. You will be as happy as happy can be, and I do most heartily rejoice it is all settled. I was quite taken by surprise, not thinking the event was so near taking place. How very good of you to sacrifice yourself one of your very few days by coming over here, and how I shall like to see you again. I quite envy all at Shrewsbury having you, though I suppose you will soon be back again at

> Maer. Jos [Joe] is as much pleased as I am, and bids me tell you so ... We were talking last night of the chances and probabilities. My best love to all at home, particularly my Father, who will be made very happy by your news.[49]

Indeed Robert was delighted, as he wrote to his brother-in-law, Jos:

> Emma having accepted Charles gives me as great happiness as Jos [Joe] having married Caroline, and I cannot say more. On that marriage Bessy said she should not have had more pleasure if it had been Victoria, and you may assure her I feel as grateful to her for Emma ... Pray give my love to Elizabeth, I fear I ought to condole with her, as the loss will be very great.[50]

Even with all the excitement, Robert could feel the burden that would now fall on Elizabeth, the remaining unmarried daughter, since her mother Bessy required constant nursing, a role that Emma had shared with Elizabeth for some time. Such sympathy was not lost on Emma, who seems to have been able to lay aside her former coolness towards her uncle, writing as a postscript in a letter from her father to Robert Darwin:

> I have begged a bit of Papa's letter to thank you from my heart for the delightful way in which you have received me into your family, and to thank my dear Marianne and Susan for their affectionate notes which gave me the greatest pleasure. One of the things that give[s] me most happiness is Charles's thorough affection and value for Papa. I am, dear Uncle, yours affectionately, Emma W.[51]

Like Joe and Caroline the year before, Charles and Emma's engagement was brief, and they were married on 20 January 1839 in the church at Maer. The happiness of the day was clouded for all the family by the knowledge that Joe and Caroline's baby, Sophy, was dying, despite Robert Darwin's best efforts to help her.[52] As Charles and Emma boarded the train to start their new life in London, they were confident of financial security, for their marriage settlement was the same as Joe and Caroline's – £10,000 from Robert Darwin, and £5,000 from Jos Wedgwood. In addition, Robert conveyed a mortgage that he had on the estates of the Mostyn Owens of Woodhouse to Charles and Emma, enabling them to enjoy the interest income for the rest of its term.[53]

Joe and Caroline, meanwhile, were also making use of their financial provision. Joe's father Jos resigned his partnership in the Wedgwood firm in 1841, and gave his permission for Joe to sell his share of the business to his brother Frank. This money, together with their marriage settlement and a bridging loan of £6,325 from Robert Darwin, enabled Joe and Caroline to buy Leith Hill Place, near Dorking in Surrey, in 1842.[54] On 17 February that year, shortly before they moved, another daughter, christened Katherine Elizabeth Sophy, but always known as Sophy, was born. Remembering the trauma surrounding her first baby, Caroline was taking no chances and returned to her father's care at The Mount to give birth, where Marianne also looked after her.[55] Charles happened to be visiting soon after and wrote, 'Caroline's morbid sensitiveness about the baby is quite fearful; she thinks every cry of the utmost importance, and I believe by night never allows the monthly nurse to change the baby's napkins, even when in bed with the monthly nurse.'[56] Her fears were groundless, since the baby grew up well, and was soon followed by two other sisters, Margaret (1843) and Lucy (1846).

12

THE SUN GOES DOWN

After all these major events, life settled into a slower rhythm at The Mount, especially since Robert's health often gave cause for concern. In 1842 Susan had turned thirty-nine, while Catherine was thirty-two. Both still entertained hopes of marriage, but by then most eligible bachelors in their circle of family and friends were already spoken for. The sisters, especially Susan, became increasingly well known in Shrewsbury for their charitable works, particularly the school, which they had taken over after Caroline's marriage. Whereas Caroline's oversight had been very much 'hands on', her younger sisters' role was more managerial. Susan did the general oversight, while Catherine dealt with the finances via her father's accounts.[1] Though the family members were now more widespread, they continued to keep in regular contact both by letter and visits. For example, Susan visited both her brothers in the winter of 1844.[2] Susan also gave furniture and other gifts to Charles and his growing family once they had moved to Down House in Kent in the autumn of 1842.[3]

Robert's health may have been failing, but his mind was as active as ever. With no significant medical work to attend to, he was able to devote his full attention to his financial affairs, which became increasingly complex.[4] He gained steady income from his longstanding investments in turnpikes and canals, and started to take out shares in the new railways. He lent £3,200 to the Trustees of the Street Act for improvements to the town, and £4,500 to help finance the new County Hall. He continued to provide unsecured loans to favoured individuals, and lent large sums to some of the great local families under mortgage agreements.[5] All of these investments were enormously profitable, as well as being secure, though cash flow could sometimes be a problem, as Charles noted in a letter in May 1846. Charles had recently bought a farm at Beesby in Lincolnshire with a loan from his father, who had also promised to lend him a further sum to erect new buildings. But Charles had to ask the agent 'to give me as long a notice as you conveniently can when you want the money … as my Father owing to some arrangements has been rather short of money this spring, but I apprehend very soon now all times will be equally convenient to him.'[6]

Robert had also lent Charles the money to buy Down House, his new home in Kent, which he repaid using part of his marriage settlement.[7] Robert treated all the children equally, giving or lending money as they needed, and most of it was paid back before Robert's death, save

County Hall, *c.* 1890. Robert Darwin lent money for its construction. (David Trumper)

some that Erasmus had borrowed. Perhaps the son felt that his needs were greater than those of his father, and certainly his father was not going to starve, since it has been calculated that in 1845 Robert Darwin lent a total of £84,049 (perhaps over £3 million by today's prices).[8] There was more than a grain of truth in the assertion made after his death that 'he owned three-quarters of Shrewsbury, and knew the medical secrets of the rest.'[9]

By 1845 Robert's health was deteriorating further, with chest infections and breathing difficulties. Being forced to sleep downstairs was a blow to his morale, but generally he remained cheerful.[10] Knowing that the end would not be too long, he started to put his affairs in order. He updated his will in September 1845, and began leaving instructions for his two sons, whom he had chosen as his executors. For example, he noted that the deeds for the Bitterley Estate were 'in the tin box under the back stairs', while Lord Berwick's deeds were 'under my bed', and the papers relating to the £40,000 he had lent the Childe family were 'in the second drawer of the bureau'.[11] He also directed that the Claythorpe Estate in Lincolnshire, which he was in the process of buying, was to 'be considered as belonging to Susan', perhaps reflecting his gratitude for her loyal commitment over many years.

By the spring of 1848, when Charles visited Shrewsbury, Robert's condition was giving great cause for 'continual anxiety', as Charles wrote to Emma, though his father was cheerful enough.[12] His nights were very bad, but he was well looked after by his manservant, Thomas Thurger, and his coachman, Mark Briggs, helped by Susan and Catherine. Charles had to go back to Down, knowing that he might never see his father alive again. And so it proved. Catherine wrote to him on Sunday 12 November:

> He is weaker and weaker, and there is no sign of rallying. Our only comfort must be that he does not suffer quite so much both yesterday and this morning, as might be … Last night was most distressing

> ... as he could not lie down on first going to bed, but was obliged to be moved back into his study ...
> He cannot speak above a whisper, and that, very short, his breathing is so difficult.
> He is perfectly collected, and placid in his mind in every way, and one of the most beautiful and pathetic sights that can be imagined. [He is] so sweet and uncomplaining, so full of everybody else, of all the servants, the servants' children etc.
>
> Susan was up all last night, and the greatest part of the night before. She is wonderfully able to go through her most trying part, all his directions being given to her. He attempted to speak about you this morning, but was so excessively overcome he was utterly unable ... Both Thurger and Mark are invaluable – they are perfectly devoted, no words can describe it. Mr Burd [a surgeon from the infirmary] and Dr [Henry] Parker both agree that nothing more can be done.[13]

Catherine's letter of the next day described the inevitable end:

> Our dear Father died this morning about half past 8. His last end was as little suffering as could be hoped with his complaint ... Susan sat close to him the whole time. Mr Burd came, but nothing could be done. The most painful part was the extreme difficulty of understanding him, from his breath being so going ... Mark and Thurger one on each side of him the whole night. Marianne and Caroline are tolerable. Poor Susan has had the most incessant trying, but she is supported by thinking she was a comfort to him. His consciousness failed latterly. But his sweetness never failed him, saying, 'thank you' several times to anything that was done in his terrible state. We must all give thanks to God that he was spared a very suffering termination of all, which he dreaded so much.
>
> God comfort you my dearest Charles. You were so beloved by him.[14]

Robert probably died of heart failure, one effect of which is that the weak heart is not able to pump body fluids normally round the body. This fluid then builds up in the legs, abdomen and especially in the lungs. These days we have powerful 'water tablets' to alleviate this, but for Robert it meant that he literally slowly drowned in the fluid building up in his lungs. To try to improve the symptoms he sat up all the time, but he could not talk and his breathing became increasingly laboured, until he finally lost consciousness. The whole process must have been terrifying, and the fear could have resulted in irritability, even anger, directed towards those who were trying to help. Yet the testimony of those who were with him at the last was just the opposite, as Catherine wrote in her letter to Charles. So he died as he had lived – a kind and courageous man.

Robert died on Monday 13 November 1848. In her letter Catherine explained to Charles that the funeral was fixed for Saturday 18, and that if he set out on the Thursday he could easily arrive in Shrewsbury in time. Susan wrote to her brother Erasmus, telling him the same. News of the great man's death spread fast, as recorded in the *Shrewsbury Chronicle*:

> Dr Parker (his son-in-law) and all the chief medical gentlemen of the town had assembled in testimony of regard, and soon spread the lamented tidings ... In the streets leading to the mansion [the Mount] the lowest cottager had darkened his windows, and the children who every morning had left the mansion (never empty-handed) stood at their own doors weeping.[15]

The news of their father's death made both brothers physically ill. Erasmus had to ask Fanny Hensleigh to accompany him to the station before he could manage to get on the train for

The New Salop Infirmary, *c.* 1850. (Henry Pidgeon, *Memorials of Shrewsbury* J.H. Leake, Shrewsbury, 1850)

Shrewsbury. Charles would have to go alone, as Emma was far advanced in pregnancy, and he felt far too ill to travel on the Thursday as he had hoped. He did manage to set off on the Friday, and spent the night at Erasmus' house in London, but by the time he arrived at Shrewsbury station the next day, the funeral was already taking place. He therefore went straight to The Mount, where he found Marianne, who was too distressed to cope with attending the service.[16]

The funeral took place at St Chad's Church, Montford, where Susannah had been buried over thirty years before. The four Parker boys were honorary pallbearers, while Joe and Caroline Wedgwood led the family mourners, with Dr Parker and Catherine following them. Erasmus, who wondered till the last minute if his nerve would hold, brought up the rear with Susan. Afterwards, when the rest of the family joined Charles and Marianne at the Mount, one after another was physically sick, such was the emotion of the day.

The family's next task was to visit Thomas Salt, the solicitor, to have the will read, and to make a start on dealing with their father's complicated financial affairs. Erasmus and Charles had been appointed executors of his will, though Charles, pleading ill health, left all the administration to his brother.[17] Each of the daughters received £10,000 cash 'to be payable in twelve calendar months after my decease, with interest at four pounds per cent from the day of my decease until the payment thereof'.[18] Writing the instruction in this way encouraged the bank to pay the money quickly, a detail that was typical of Robert's financial acumen. Erasmus received £15,500 in cash, and Charles £20,000. Curiously, the amount for Charles was written in the margin of the will – presumably this was just a scribal error, not second thoughts on his father's part. The two sons were also left the lands in Lincolnshire that Robert had inherited from his

Montford Church and the Darwin grave. (Author's collection)

maternal grandfather. These attracted significant amounts of rental income. The Mount, with all its associated properties and lands, was left to Susan and Catherine, provided they remained single and in residence. It is hard to make comparisons, but the value of the monetary gifts alone would probably be in excess of £2 million at today's prices, without any consideration of the property and land. When all his affairs were finally sorted his total estate was £223,759, around £9 million today.[19] No wonder none of the children had any future financial worries. Later, Erasmus assigned the mortgage income from some of the loans that his father had made to Joe and Caroline, Susan and himself. Over the ensuing forty years or so, as the older generation died, some of this income was in turn passed on to the children of Joe and Caroline and Charles and Emma.[20]

Much as the children appreciated their financial windfall, money would never be able to compensate for the loss of their father. In time they would come to terms with his not being there in the flesh, but somehow his larger-than-life personality would always be with them. Charles longed to talk about him, and many of his letters over the ensuing weeks indicate the depth of his loss. For example, he wrote to his agent in Lincolnshire, 'Although you do not allude to the great loss we have experienced in the death of my Father, I am well assured, from what I have heard you say, that you will sympathise with us. A man with more entire kindness of heart could not, I am certain, exist ... '[21] A couple of months later he wrote to his cousin, W.D Fox, 'I saw two very nice notes of yours on the occasion of my poor dear Father's death. The memory of such a Father is a treasure to one, and when last I saw him he was very comfortable and his expression which I have now in my mind's eye serene and cheerful.'[22]

Soon after Robert's death, Susan and Catherine paid a visit to Charles and Emma at Down, and the following March Charles went off to Malvern for 'hydropathic' treatment for his recurring illnesses. He wrote to Susan from there: 'My dearest sisters, I wish I could see you here. I saw absolutely nothing of you at Down, and never talked about my dear Father, about whom it is now to me the sweetest pleasure to think, which I fear cannot be your case as yet.'[23] Later that month he wrote to his friend Joseph Hooker: 'I have had a bad winter. On the 13th of November my poor dear Father died, and no one who did not know him would believe that a man above 83 years old [he was actually 82] could have retained so tender and affectionate a disposition, with all his sagacity unclouded to the last.'[24]

13

THE END OF AN ERA

The years after Robert Darwin's death were challenging in many ways for his six children. Charles' illness was at its worst, and he was struggling with his scientific work. His monumental study of barnacles seemed to go on forever, and he continued to doubt if his work on 'the species problem' would stand up to professional and public scrutiny. Home life, too, was increasingly busy with new arrivals. Yet even though Emma seemed to be forever pregnant or nursing small babies, she still had time to support and encourage her husband. Charles and Emma would be drawn even closer in the next challenge they faced.

It concerned Anne (or Annie, as they always called her), their eldest daughter, who was born in 1841. In the summer of 1850 Charles and Emma realised that there was something seriously wrong with her health, and despite their best efforts, she continued to deteriorate through the following winter.[1] By March 1851 she was not improving, and they feared she had consumption (tuberculosis). In desperation they decided to take Annie to Malvern for Dr Gully's water cure, but Charles had to accompany his daughter by himself, since Emma was too far advanced in pregnancy to travel. Sensing the seriousness of the situation, the family rallied round. Fanny Hensleigh left her children with Joe and Caroline at Leith Hill Place and rushed to be with Charles in Malvern, while two of Emma's elderly aunts hurried to Down to be with her. Charles and Emma's seven-year-old daughter Etty (Henrietta) joined her cousins with Joe and Caroline, who promised the parents that 'they shall never be long out of my sight or hearing ... They are all gone cowslip gathering in the fields.'[2]

Soon afterwards it fell to Caroline to tell Etty the awful news – her sister, 'the joy of the household', as her father called her, was dead.[3] For Caroline it must have brought back memories of trying to explain the death of their mother to Charles when he was about the same age as Etty. Hensleigh Wedgwood travelled to Malvern to help Fanny with the funeral arrangements, and they persuaded Charles to return to Down before the funeral day. Although Charles and Emma had each other's company, their inability to be at their daughter's funeral must have added to their grief. This is evidenced by Charles' words to his brother Erasmus two days after Annie's death: 'Poor Emma is well bodily and very firm, but feels bitterly and God knows we can neither see on any side a gleam of comfort.'[4]

The whole wider family felt the loss of Annie. Catherine had not been able to go to

Anne Darwin. (English Heritage)

Malvern from Shrewsbury because she was ill, but both she and Susan hastened to send their condolences as soon as they heard the news of Annie's death. Susan wrote, 'I must tell you how we grieve for you and earnestly pray you may both be comforted under this bitter affliction … Poor Catherine has been entirely laid up since Sunday evening, and is not yet out of her room. She was exceedingly grieved not to have gone on Thursday [before Annie's death], but doubts now if she could have done so … I shall ever mourn the dearest child I ever knew, and most dearly I loved her.'[5] Catherine wrote in a similar vein, 'I can only hope that God may comfort you in your great sorrow … It is an infinite mercy to think that your Darling did not suffer … You know how we loved her – her sweet and affectionate ways are before me all day.'[6]

Catherine wrote to Charles at greater length a couple of days later:

> I wished very much to have thanked you yesterday for your great kindness in writing to me – I was so anxious to hear of you and poor, poor Emma. Her sweet note is come this morning to Susan; the loss of your poor darling is the most heart-rending grief that has ever happened to this family. I did not like to tell you in my last (but may now) how often Susan and I have been thankful that my Father was spared this great grief – it would have been such agitation and distress to him, besides such sorrow. I think it must be some comfort to you both, to think that as long as her little life was granted you, you both did everything in the world to make her happy. No little dear could have had a happier life except [for] her health, till her little innocent spirit was called above. Caroline used to say long ago (when alarmed about Sophy) that her great consolation would be, if she lost her, to think that her life had been as happy as she could make it.[7]

So the family pulled together, and sought to comfort one another in Charles and Emma's loss, which they all felt so acutely.

It may be that the whole incident especially affected Caroline, since around that time she started to show signs of serious mental illness. She began to neglect her appearance and abandoned the running of her house. Gradually she became more and more of a recluse, not leaving Leith Hill Place for months at a time.[8] Of course, it is hard to know at this distance what was wrong, but my guess is that it was a very severe depression. We have already noted that Charles commented on her excessive anxiety when her daughter Sophy was a baby, which may have been a symptom of post-natal depression.[9] Another precipitating factor in a depressive illness may have been her husband Joe's inability to demonstrate affection. At this period he seems to have become increasingly autocratic – perhaps he felt he had to act out the part of the country squire he had become. For example, his three young daughters had to stand in line each day to receive their treat, a spoonful of cream, provided that they had been well behaved.[10] Another possible factor in Caroline's mental condition may have been anxiety over her daughter Sophy, who was becoming increasingly 'odd', perhaps as a result of an autistic tendency. It appears that Joe took Caroline to Sir Benjamin Brodie, who had recently published *Psychological Inquiries*, but he seemed to be of little help.[11] A niece recorded in 1864 that her Aunt Caroline was still 'eccentric and secretive',[12] but in the end her illness remitted spontaneously, and seems not to have returned.

The 1850s were not good for the Parkers, either. Henry resigned as a physician at the Salop Infirmary in 1850, after just four years on the staff. Whether he continued in medical practice after that is not known, and he died at Overton in January 1856, aged sixty-eight. Marianne died two years later, in July 1858, aged just sixty. By this time the five Parker children were all in their twenties or early thirites. Robert was thirty-three – there is no record of his life after this date. Henry was thirty-one, and already a Fellow of Oriel College, Oxford, and a fine-art specialist. Frank was twenty-nine, and a solicitor in Chester, while Charles was twenty-seven and had just obtained an MA from University College, Oxford. He then went on to be ordained, becoming vicar of Ford, a village just west of Shrewsbury, from 1863-70. Mary was twenty-two and living at home. The two youngest children may have made their home at The

The grave of Henry and Marianne Parker in Overton Churchyard. (Author's collection)

Mount after their parents died, since they are recorded there in the census of 1861 (though they may have just been visiting). In 1866 Mary married Edward Mostyn Owen of Woodhouse, near Rednal, whose family were long-time friends of the Darwins.

The publication of *The Origin of Species* meant that 1859 was a momentous year for Charles. He sent copies to all his siblings, and Caroline's mental health was good enough for her to read the book with understanding, writing back a very complimentary letter to Charles, though she had some minor reservations which she detailed. He replied that, 'I am astounded that you care as much for my Book as you seem to do. Your doubt and queries are perfectly correct … '[13] Quite what made him so astounded that she liked it we cannot know. Perhaps he thought that her deep religious convictions would make her critical of the conclusions of the book, but it may have been that her Unitarian background made her tolerant of such views.

Erasmus was totally bowled over by the book, despite having discussed the contents with his brother on many occasions. He wrote, 'I really think it is the most interesting book I ever read, and can only compare it to the first knowledge of chemistry, getting into a new world, or rather behind the scenes. To me the geographical distribution … is the most convincing of the proofs, and the relation of the oldest forms to the existing species. I dare say I don't feel enough the absence of varieties [intermediate forms in the fossil record], but then I don't in the least know if everything now living were fossilized whether the palaeontologists could distinguish them. In fact the *a priori* reasoning is so entirely satisfactory to me that if the facts won't fit in, why, so much the worse for the facts, is my feeling.'[14] One may wryly comment that 'the facts', or the interpretation of them, have been a bone of contention ever since!

We do not know what Susan and Catherine thought of *The Origin of Species*, but one copy found its way into the library at The Mount.[15] The library was a resource they often used, for life had become increasingly quiet in the family home since their father had died. They had the school, though, to keep them occupied, and many of the children in the locality were in the habit of knocking on the door for small treats. They also had a steady stream of visitors, such as an annual visit from the Hensleigh Wedgwoods, though this was not an occasion that the Wedgwood children looked forward to with any enthusiasm. Their dislike of The Mount was mainly down to Catherine's character. One of the Hensleigh Wedgwood girls wrote to another in August 1858 that, 'what is trying in Catherine is not so much any actual fault of temper, as unreasonable lamentations over what cannot be helped – exaggerated fits of dislike to trifling things to which a careful easy companion who takes things lightly would not much mind.'[16] Which probably means in modern language that she moaned a lot! Catherine especially bemoaned her lack of status. Though both Susan and she were unmarried, Susan was head of the household, in charge of the school and somewhat of a local celebrity, whereas Catherine had none of these roles.

Her situation, however, was soon to change. In 1863 she scandalised some of her family, especially the Wedgwoods, by announcing her engagement to Revd Charles Langton. What caused offence was the fact that Langton's first wife was Charlotte Wedgwood, Emma's older sister, who had died just the previous year.[17] Charlotte Wedgwood and Charles Langton had been married in 1832 after a whirlwind courtship. Langton became vicar of Onibury in south Shropshire, but by 1842 had lost his faith to such an extent that he resigned his living. Then he, Charlotte and their young son moved back to Charlotte's family home, Maer Hall in Staffordshire, to care for Charlotte's mother, Bessy. When the latter died in 1846, Maer Hall was sold, and the Langtons moved to Hartfield Grove in Sussex.

Catherine Darwin and Charles Langton were married in London in the autumn of 1863, and settled in Shrewsbury, though not back at The Mount.[18] Both Catherine and Charles Langton are described as being 'strong-willed, quick tempered and depressive',[19] so one wonders how their marriage fared, but in the event it was not to last for long. By late 1865 it was clear that Catherine was seriously ill, possibly with some form of cancer or leukaemia,[20] and she moved back to the familiarity of The Mount, where she could be cared for. Early in the New Year she managed one last letter to Charles and Emma:

> I am so rapidly weaker I can lose no time in sending you all and Elizabeth [Emma's sister, who lived near Charles and Emma] my dearest farewell. It is grievous to think I shall never see any of your dear faces. On New Year's day I knew this, and what a different world it seems to me.
>
> What I want to say is that poor Susan feels my loss so cruelly - I left off this last night as I was too exhausted to go on.
>
> I am grieved indeed at poor Susan's loneliness, but there seems no help.
>
> My dearest husband will feel my loss too; what a nurse he is, if he was not deaf.
>
> Everybody's love and goodness to me are past speech.
>
> May God bless you all, and may we meet hereafter.[21]

Catherine died on 1 February, with Sophia Kerry, one of the servants at The Mount, present at the moment of death.[22] She was aged just fifty-five, and was interred in the family grave at Montford. Twice-bereaved Charles Langton remained a widower for another eighteen years, when he married for a third time aged eighty-four. He died four years later.[23]

Erasmus was left to sort out how Susan would pay Catherine's estate for the possessions at the Mount that had been left to them jointly by their father.[24] He suggested that nothing should be done about it until after Susan's death, perhaps because by then the family realised that Susan, too, was seriously ill. Her health had begun to cause concern to the family in the autumn of 1865.[25] She also realised that the situation was serious, and she was particularly anxious to ensure that the school would continue in the event of her death. The obvious way forward was to ask the trustees of Millington's Hospital to take over running the school. So she wrote in mid-December, asking 'that after her death its maintenance be secured.'[26] The trustees deferred the decision until their February meeting, but then the answer was 'no' – the hospital's charter didn't allow for the care of under six-year-olds, and if they took on the over sixes they would exceed the numbers allowed by the foundation.[27] In the end, the Darwins' school was incorporated into St George's Church of England School nearby in 1868, which in time became part of the state system.[28]

Susan's medical problem was persistent bleeding from the uterus, presumably due to cancer.[29] Over the ensuing months she gradually deteriorated, until Charles could write in late September, 'My poor sister lives, but is dying. It is a great comfort that she has now ceased suffering and dozes nearly all day long. She wishes, poor thing, earnestly for death, and really death is nothing compared to much suffering. It will soon now all be over.'[30] Which indeed it was, the end occurring on 3 October, with the faithful Jane Grice in attendance. Jane was sixty-five by then, and had been housekeeper for the Darwins for at least twenty-five years, though in all probability longer. Born in Rodington, north-east of Shrewsbury, she never married, giving the bulk of her life to the service of this one family.[31] Susan, the down-to-earth pragmatist, would be sorely missed, not least by Erasmus, who regarded her as his favourite amongst the four sisters.[32] Charles also was greatly saddened. Writing to a Shrewsbury friend he said, 'The loss of my poor sister, Susan, has been a great one to many …'[33]

After eighty years there were suddenly no more Darwins in Shrewsbury. Under Robert's will, The Mount and its contents were to be shared amongst the surviving children once the unmarried sisters had died. So Caroline, Erasmus and Charles had the melancholy task of disposing of everything. In this they were helped by Henry and Frank Parker, the executors of Susan's will. Caroline and Erasmus were staying at The Mount at the time of Susan's death, and before he left for home Erasmus collected up 'an immense big box' of letters, especially those that Charles had written from the *Beagle*.[34, 35] He wrote to Charles, 'I will keep them for a time for the chance of having energy to look at them, and then you can have them.'[36] Caroline had a few of their father's letters, and tried to sort out various queries about the silver, but her poor health made it impossible to do much more. Erasmus was very worried about her. Just after Susan's death he wrote to Charles, 'Caroline is looking very much worn, and it is a great mercy that she did not break down altogether just at last. It has been a most painful time.'[37] A week later he added, 'I never saw anything so miserably ill as Caroline is looking. She is tired of her present doctor, and I recommended Paget, and she is going to consult him. She seems to suffer most severe pain.'[38] (The 'Paget' referred to was Sir James Paget, one of the most eminent doctors of the day, and an expert on arthritic complaints. Caroline evidently suffered severely from some form of arthritis.)

Charles, ill again, appears not even to have made it to the funeral, and none of the three remaining siblings had the heart to do anything more about The Mount and its possessions.

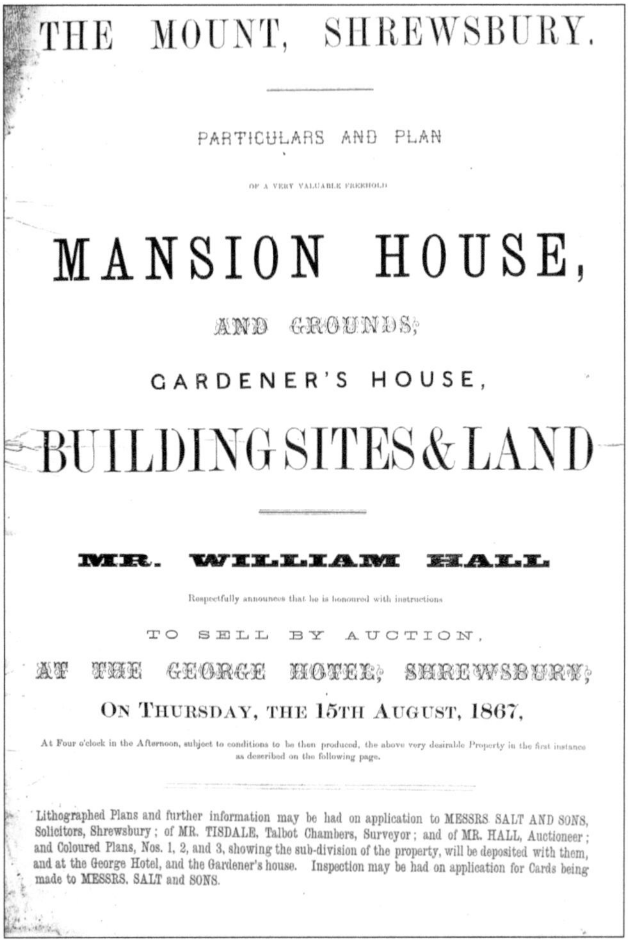

THE MOUNT, SHREWSBURY.

PARTICULARS AND PLAN

OF A VERY VALUABLE FREEHOLD

MANSION HOUSE,

AND GROUNDS;

GARDENER'S HOUSE,

BUILDING SITES & LAND

MR. WILLIAM HALL

Respectfully announces that he is honoured with instructions

TO SELL BY AUCTION,

AT THE GEORGE HOTEL, SHREWSBURY;

ON THURSDAY, THE 15TH AUGUST, 1867,

At Four o'clock in the Afternoon, subject to conditions to be then produced, the above very desirable Property in the first instance as described on the following page.

Lithographed Plans and further information may be had on application to MESSRS SALT AND SONS, Solicitors, Shrewsbury; of MR. TISDALE, Talbot Chambers, Surveyor; and of MR. HALL, Auctioneer; and Coloured Plans, Nos. 1, 2, and 3, showing the sub-division of the property, will be deposited with them, and at the George Hotel, and the Gardener's house. Inspection may be had on application for Cards being made to MESSRS. SALT and SONS.

Sale catalogue for The Mount, 1867. (Shrewsbury Museums Service)

The rest of the priceless collection of Wedgwood that Susannah had lovingly collected all those years before was offered to any member of the family who would take it, and all the remaining items were hastily put up for auction.[39]

The sale of the house contents lasted six days – Monday to Saturday, 19-24 November 1866.[40] Amongst the items highlighted were 1,120oz of silver-plated articles, at least five complete sets of Wedgwood china of various types, cut glass, antique china and so on. The library contents are interesting. There were Dr Darwin's old medical books, and his Royal Society dissertation. There was also his father Erasmus' *Botanic Garden*, and Anna Seward's *Life of Erasmus Darwin* (perhaps Robert had forgiven her for what she had written about his father). Then there was Charles' *Voyage of the Beagle* and *The Origin of Species*, and many other more popular works of the period. Towards the end of the list was a lot entitled, '11 volumes of the rights of women, pamphlets etc.' Presumably those belonged to Susan and Catherine, suggesting that they had inherited some of their mother's feminist interests.

All the items from the main reception room, twelve bedrooms, servants' quarters and all the outhouses were sold in turn. You could have bought four carriages, nine tons of hay, a pig, and even the family dog! Not only the house contents, but also anything portable from the garden was sold. The sale of plants and garden equipment provides a snapshot into garden history, and has been well documented.[41]

Astonishingly, the total for the sale of all these items was less than £1,500.[42] The sale of the house was no more successful, as there were no bidders when it was put up for auction on 30 November 1866. The house was re-advertised and auctioned off in August 1867, being bought by Edward Lowe, the owner of an adjacent property. He did not live in The Mount himself, but leased it to others.[43] Also auctioned off were the coachman's house and the gardener's house, both nearby. Erasmus kindly arranged that Mark Briggs, the coachman, and Wynne the gardener would continue to be provided for, even after his own death.[44]

So ended the era of the Darwins in Shrewsbury. The three remaining siblings were deeply saddened that the house and all it stood for would now be just a memory. Charles felt this particularly, perhaps because he had not been at Susan's funeral. So, in 1869, two years after The Mount was sold, Charles asked his daughter Henrietta (Etty) to go to Shrewsbury with him so that he could see the old house one last time. He stood in the house and tried to conjure up the past, but the new owner kept talking and would not leave him alone.[45] As it did not belong to the Darwins any more, Charles could hardly ask the man to go away. Later, when they were leaving, Charles said to his daughter, 'If I could have been left alone in that green-house for five minutes, I know I should have been able to see my father in his wheelchair as vividly as if he had been there before me.'[46]

It all seemed a sad anticlimax to the story of the Darwins in Shrewsbury. But in time, once they recovered from the triple blow of losing the two sisters and the house in such a short space of time, Caroline, Erasmus and Charles would view things in a much more positive light. The people of Shrewsbury, too, would remember many good things about the last years of the Darwins in their town. For example, an obituary in the local paper recorded the death of Susan as follows:

> Our obituary of this day records the death of this amiable and truly estimable lady. Her loss will be truly felt by all the poor who resided within a large circle round her hospitable residence, to whom she has for many years dispensed her charities with a warm heart and generous hand. Recognising the importance of the very young children of hard-working poor parents being cared for and instructed, she, in conjunction with her sister, established an infant school in Frankwell, which, for some years past, has been maintained at her sole cost. Besides this she was a liberal donor to the charitable institutions of the town, and her death will leave a void which will not be easily filled up.[47]

In the same vein, a local historian, who knew both sisters, wrote that 'both of them were exceedingly charitable ladies and were greatly missed in the suburb of Frankwell by the poor.'[48] That may have been the end of the life and work of the Darwins in Shrewsbury, but it certainly was not the end of the Darwins of Shrewsbury. The focus of their lives was now in the south of England.

EPILOGUE

If the era of the Darwins in Shrewsbury ended on a rather downbeat note, the final years of the remaining Shrewsbury siblings, Charles, Erasmus and Caroline, were generally more positive. Though each was busy with their own lives, they continued to keep in touch as they grew older. Charles, of course, was already well on his way to international fame. This part of his life has been well documented elsewhere, and is not really relevant to our story, so will not be detailed further.

Erasmus, or 'poor dear old Ras', as his friend Thomas Carlyle rather unkindly called him, continued to spend his life in 'patient idleness'.[1] The highlight of most days was a visit to the Hensleigh Wedgwoods, where he would enjoy spending time with his dearest friend Fanny and surrogate children Hope and Effie, whom he called his 'wee wife', and 'our children'.[2] The Hensleigh Wedgwoods were also close to the Charles Darwins, and sometimes Erasmus would join the two families at Down. Charles and Hensleigh, whose obsession and love of research drew them together, enjoyed intellectual arguments about anything and everything, especially religion.

In the 1860s and 1870s there was a great interest in spiritualism. One winter evening in 1874 Erasmus thought it would be good entertainment to have a séance, so he arranged one at his house, to which he invited, among others, the Charles Darwins and the Hensleigh Wedgwoods.[3] Charles found the whole thing thoroughly unpleasant and escaped from the room, but the Hensleigh Wedgwoods were much more convinced. Although earlier in their lives they had been evangelical Christians, they now became involved in spiritualism. Hensleigh was also one of the founder members of the Society for Psychical Research.[4] Erasmus continued to hold séances, and appears to have had more than a passing interest in spiritualism. As he grew older his behaviour became increasingly affected, such as often carrying a small kitten in his waistcoat pocket.[5]

By the 1870s Caroline had recovered from her mental illness, and, though still badly affected by arthritis and now also suffering from heart disease, she enjoyed a period of greater contentment. Joe, too, although he was pushing eighty, was enjoying his family, which now included grandchildren.[6] Most of the time their three daughters continued to live at Leith Hill Place. Sophy, becoming increasingly eccentric, was there, of course. Lucy, the third daughter,

Charles Darwin aged sixty-two, from the *Illustrated London News*, March 1871. (Shrewsbury Museums Service)

married a sailor, so was often at home when her husband was away at sea. Margaret, the second daughter, had married Revd Arthur Vaughan Williams, vicar of Down Ampney, Gloucestershire. They had three children – Hervey (born 1869), Margaret (born 1870), and Ralph (born 1872). Sadly, however, Arthur died in 1875, leaving Margaret a widow at the age of thirty-two. So Margaret and the three small children moved back from Gloucestershire to Leith Hill Place.

Joe Wedgwood died peacefully in March 1880, aged eighty-five. Though it is easy to paint him in a rather negative light because of his extreme reserve, he was a very loving man, esteemed by the rest of the wider family. He and Caroline's marriage had been generally happy, especially considering that he had had to cope with her mental illness.[7] Caroline certainly missed him dreadfully, a void which Charles and Emma sought to fill, both by visiting her in Surrey and by inviting her to Down. During one visit, Caroline expressed the wish to see Erasmus again, for it was clear that he, too, was far from well. So, despite her poor health, she travelled up to London with her daughter Margaret, and on Saturday 20 August 1881 she and Erasmus reminisced about old times at The Mount. In the event her visit was only just in time, for the following day Erasmus was taken ill again, a relapse from which he did not recover, and he died the following Friday. When he was taken ill Fanny Hensleigh was away, and the family feared that he might die before she returned, but she arrived back in time, and was able to stay with him until he died, which is what he wanted most of all. The Darwin family had long since ceased worrying about the possible scandal surrounding the relationship between Erasmus and Fanny – this arrangement seemed to suit all concerned. Caroline had not realised that Fanny had been with Erasmus when he died, and so she wrote to Fanny, 'It is hard on you [not to have been with him at the end] who have made the happiness of his life.'[8]

Erasmus was buried at Downe Church (in the village near Down House). His epitaph, written by Carlyle, read, 'One of the sincerest, truest, and most modest of men'.[9] Julia (Snow) Wedgwood, one of his 'adopted' nieces, wrote an obituary of him in the *Spectator*. She described his playfulness, tenderness, humour, lightness of touch and 'the peculiar mixture of something pathetic with a sort of gay scorn, entirely remote from contempt ... Erasmus Darwin has passed away in old age, yet his memory retains something of a youthful fragrance; his influence gives much happiness of a kind usually associated with youth to many lives ... '[10]

She also wrote that his life seemed 'something less than it ought to have been', which could hardly have been said of his brother Charles. By this time, Charles too was obviously ailing, and shortly after his brother died he had his first heart attack. His heart condition worsened steadily and on 19 April 1882 he quietly passed away, with Emma holding his hand. He was feted by the great and good at a state funeral a week later, but Emma chose not to go, since she had already said her goodbyes.[11]

After Charles' death, his family found amongst his voluminous papers his autobiography, which he wrote during the period 1876-79, expressly stating that he did not write it for publication, but just for the benefit of his family. However, it was perhaps inevitable that what such a famous person had written about himself would not remain private forever. And so it proved. Articles began to appear by those who knew him,[12] and for some time the family debated amongst themselves as to whether the autobiography should be published. Eventually, perhaps to ensure that the record was kept 'straight', they decided to print it. Emma found some of what Charles had written distressing, since it expressed negative views on various people, especially family members, and about the Christianity she held dear, and consequentially she and her son Francis (Frank) edited out the parts that they did not wish the public to see. This edition appeared in the autumn of 1887.

Leith Hill Place, home of Joe and Caroline Wedgwood. (Originally published in Wedgwood, Barbara and Hensleigh, *The Wedgwood Circle* Studio Vista, 1980 – reproduced courtesy of Sir Martin Wedgwood)

In the years after Charles' death, his sister Caroline lived quietly at Leith Hill Place. Though increasingly disabled, her mind was still active, so Emma Darwin decided to send her a copy of the published version of the autobiography. Most of the family members were happy with the book, but Caroline felt a bit differently, especially about Charles' childhood and his relationship with their father. She must have felt sad when Charles wrote that he was a naughty boy,[13] for her recollection was quite different. She remembered that, 'instead of being "a naughty boy" [Charles] was particularly affectionate, tractable and sweet tempered.'[14]

She was particularly concerned, though, with the impression that the book gave of Robert Darwin. Not knowing that Emma and Frank had deleted much of what Charles had written about their father, it must have seemed strange to her that the only two passages in the book describing the relationship between father and son showed his father in a rather poor light. The passage Caroline was most unhappy about was:

> To my deep mortification my father once said to me, 'You care for nothing but shooting, dogs and rat-catching, and you will be a disgrace to yourself and all your family.' But my father, who was the kindest man I ever knew, and whose memory I love with all my heart, must have been angry and somewhat unjust when he used such words.[15]

She felt so strongly that she wrote back to Emma as follows:

> I wish some years ago I had known that Charles thought my father did not understand or know what ability and power of mind he really had. He was so proud as well as fond of him – but I often

> felt afraid that Erasmus might feel mortified and feel undervalued. I long to strike a pen through that mistaken sentence of my father's estimation of Charles.[16]

Perhaps Caroline could sense that the autobiography would tarnish Robert Darwin's reputation in the eyes of those who did not know him as intimately as she had. There were understandable reasons why Emma and Frank had omitted most of the positive things about Robert Darwin that Charles had written, since these passages described patients and others who would still be recognisable to some, even forty years after the events. Unfortunately, but probably inadvertently, the book as originally published tended to foster a belief that Robert Darwin was an overbearing and unreasonable father.[17]

Just three months later, in the bitter cold of January 1888, Caroline died, surrounded by her family at Leith Hill Place. Her death ended almost exactly a century of the association of the Darwins and Shrewsbury. It was now time for the legacy of the Shrewsbury Darwins to be passed to succeeding generations. And what a legacy it turned out to be! We have already mentioned Marianne's second son Henry Parker, for many years a fellow of Oriel College Oxford and a specialist in the fine arts.

Four of Charles' sons became even more distinguished. George Darwin (1845-1912), Professor of Astronomy and Experimental Philosophy at Cambridge, was knighted, and elected a Fellow of the Royal Society (FRS). Francis (Frank) Darwin (1848-1925) studied natural sciences at Cambridge, then graduated in medicine, but never practised. He became a well-known botanist, and was also knighted and elected FRS. He edited his father's autobiography and later did the same with his letters. Major Leonard Darwin (1850-1943) was a soldier, Liberal MP for Lichfield in 1892-95, economist, eugenicist and mentor of the statistician and evolutionary biologist Ronald Fisher. Horace Darwin (1851-1928) founded the Cambridge Scientific Instrument Co. in 1885, and became mayor of Cambridge in 1896/7. He was a Fellow of Trinity College, was also elected FRS, and was knighted in 1918.

Perhaps Caroline's legacy is the most surprising. Her youngest grandson, Ralph, showed a musical ability at an early age. He was taught initially by his aunt, Sophy, who, despite her mental illness, was a talented musician.[18] This suggests that her problem was what we would now consider a variety of autism or Asperger's Syndrome – gifting in one area of life associated with difficulty in relating to others. The Darwin cousins, who like their father were an unmusical lot, thought Ralph had no talent, but after studying at Cambridge University he attended the Royal College of Music. He became, as Ralph Vaughan Williams, one of the most celebrated English composers of the twentieth century. He and his sister Margaret (Maggie) established the Leith Hill Music Festival in 1905, and he later donated the house to the National Trust.[19]

Perhaps some of Ralph's musical genes came from his great grandmother, Susannah Darwin, who was such a talented musician, and who all those years before enjoyed playing the organ at The Mount, which Robert had bought her for £200. Every time I listen to one of my favourite pieces of music, 'The Lark Ascending' by Ralph Vaughan Williams, I am grateful for that unexpected legacy from the Shrewsbury Darwins.

TIMELINE OF MAJOR EVENTS IN THE LIVES OF THE DARWINS OF SHREWSBURY

1786	Dr Robert Darwin arrives in Shrewsbury, setting up practice in St John's Hill
1796	(April) – Robert Darwin and Susannah Wedgwood marry in London. They set up house at The Crescent
1798	(April) – Marianne born
1799	Darwin family move into The Mount
1800	(September) – Caroline born
1803	(August) – Susan born
1804	(December) – Erasmus born
1809	(February) – Charles born
1810	(May) – Catherine born
1817	(spring) – Charles starts at Revd Case's school, Claremont Hill
1817	(July) – Susannah dies. Buried at St Chad's, Montford
1818	(summer) – Charles joins Erasmus at Shrewsbury School
1822	Erasmus leaves Shrewsbury School for Cambridge University
1823/4	Caroline starts infant school in Frankwell
1824	(November) – Marianne marries Dr Henry Parker at St Chad's Church, Shrewsbury
1825	(October) – Charles leaves Shrewsbury School and joins Erasmus at Edinburgh University to study medicine
1826	Erasmus qualifies in medicine, settles in London
1827	Charles leaves Edinburgh
1828	Charles starts at Cambridge University
1831	Charles obtains an ordinary degree from Cambridge

1831	(December)-1836 (October) – the voyage of the *Beagle*, after which Charles moves to London
1837	(August) – Caroline marries Josiah Wedgwood III at St George's Church, Frankwell. They settle first in Staffordshire, then Leith Hill Place, Surrey
1839	(January) – Charles marries Emma Wedgwood at Maer, Staffordshire. They settle first in London, then Down House, Kent
1848	(November) – Robert Darwin dies. Buried at Montford
1856	(January) – Dr Henry Parker dies at Overton
1858	(July) – Marianne Parker dies at Overton
1859	Charles publishes *The Origin of Species*
1863	(October) – Catherine marries Revd Charles Langton in London. They settle in Shrewsbury, but not at The Mount
1866	(February) – Catherine dies. Buried at Montford
1866	(October) – Susan dies. Buried at Montford
1866	(November) – The contents of The Mount are sold
1867	(August) – The Mount is sold
1881	(August) – Erasmus dies in London
1882	(April) – Charles dies at Down
1888	(January) – Caroline dies at Leith Hill Place

REFERENCES AND ENDNOTES

References

Abbreviations used in the references –
'Autobiography' refers to Charles Darwin's *Autobiography*, with the edition specified in the endnote
DAR refers to the Darwin papers in the Cambridge University Library
DCP – Darwin Correspondence Project, www.darwinproject.ac.uk/darwinletters
Mic – Microfilm
SA – Shropshire Archives
SC – *Shrewsbury Chronicle*

Occasionally I have 'tidied up' quotations where either the language is archaic or the spelling or punctuation is so awkward that it is difficult to read. This is especially the case with letters, which were often written in a hurry and obviously not intended for publication.

The following books, articles and websites are referred to with just the name of the author and page number in the endnotes. Other references are given in full.

Alcock, George, *Millington's Hospital, A Brief History* (Private publication, 2007)
Bellamy, Vivien, *The Making of Shrewsbury* (Wharncliffe, 2004)
Bevan, H., *Records of the Salop Infirmary, 1847*, SA D21.3 (5389/2) It is mostly unpaginated
Boyd, Peter D.A., 'The Darwin Family and their Plants at The Mount in Shrewsbury', www.peterboyd.com/darwingard3.htm (2006)
Broadbent, Arnold, *The Story of Unitarianism in Shrewsbury* (Private publication 1962, available from the Unitarian Church)
Browne, Janet, *Charles Darwin: Voyaging*, (Pimlico, 2003)
Cragg, Gerald R., *The Church and the Age of Reason*, 1648-1789 (Penguin Books, 1988)
Darwin, Charles, *Autobiography* (Thinker's Library edition, 1929)
Darwin, Charles, *Autobiography* (Penguin Classics edition, 2002)
De Saulles, Mary, *The Book of Shrewsbury* (Barracuda, 1986)
Desmond, Adrian and Moore, James, *Darwin* (Penguin, 1991)
Downes, Sara, 'Significant or Limited? The impact of the Salop Infirmary on its associated medical profession, 1745-92', OU Thesis (September 2005) SA D21.9 v.f. 18562/1
Fisher, George W., *Annals of Shrewsbury School* (Methuen, 1899)

Garner, Lawrence, The Buildings of Shropshire, Vol. III, *The Georgian and Regency Legacy, 1730-1840*, (Swan Hill Press, 1990)
Gould, Stephen Jay, 'Darwin's Deceptive Memories', *New Scientist*, 21.2.1980, pp577-579
Healey, Edna, *Emma Darwin: The Inspirational Wife of a Genius* (Review, 2001)
Hobbs, John L., 'The Haycocks Changed to Face of Shrewsbury', *Shropshire Magazine* (Feb.1960)
Howie, W.B., 'The Administration of an Eighteenth-Century Provincial Hospital: The Royal Salop Infirmary, 1747-1830', *Medical History*, Vol. 5, 1961, pp34-55
Hubble, Douglas, 'The Evolution of Charles Darwin', *Horizon, Vol. XIV*, no 80, pp75-85 (August 1946)
King-Hele, Desmond, *Erasmus Darwin*, (DLM press, 1999)
Meteyard, Eliza, *A Group of Englishmen* (Longmans, Green & Co, 1871)
Morriss, Richard and Hoverd, Ken, *The Buildings of Shrewsbury* (Alan Sutton, 1993)
Oldham, J. Basil, *A History of Shrewsbury School, 1552-1952* (Basil Blackwell, Oxford, 1952)
Phillips, W., 'The Darwins', *Shropshire Men*, Vol 4, p.13ff, SA Mic 166
Porter, Dorothy and Roy, *Patient's Progress* (Polity Press, 1989)
Posner, E., 'William Withering vs. The Darwins', *History of Medicine*, 1975, vol. 6, 51-57
Quinn, Henri, *Charles Darwin, Shrewsbury's Man of the Millennium* (Private publication, 1999)
Royle's *Manual of Materia Medica and Therapeutics*, sixth edition (J&A Churchill, 1876)
The New Dictionary of Theology, Inter-Varsity Press, 1988
Trinder, Barrie, *A History of Shropshire* (Phillimore, 1983)
Trinder, Barrie, *Beyond the Bridges, The Suburbs of Shrewsbury 1760-1960* (Phillimore, 2006)
Wedgwood, Barbara and Hensleigh, *The Wedgwood Circle* (Studio Vista, 1980)
Woodall, Edward, 'Charles Darwin', *Trans Shrops Arch and Nat Hist Soc.*, Vol.VIII, 1885, pp1-64
Woodall, R.D., *Midland Unitarianism and its Story*, 1662-1962 (Private publication) SA C98.8

Additional Sources for Illustrations
Auden, Thomas, *Shrewsbury: A Historical and Topographical Account of the Town* (Methuen, 1923)
Hulbert, Charles, *The History and Description of the County of Salop* (Private Publication, 1837)
Pattison, Andrew, *On Severn Shore* (Barnabas Community Church, Shrewsbury, 2004)
Pidgeon, Henry, *Memorials of Shrewsbury* (JH Leake, Shrewsbury, 1850)

Endnotes

Prologue

1. She was christened Susannah, but known as Sukey as a child. In adult life she was often called Susan, which is the name on her memorial. I have used the name Susannah throughout the book to avoid confusion with her daughter Susan
2. SC, 3.2.1809
3. Ibid
4. SC, 10.2.1809
5. SC., 3.3.1809
6. SC, 3.2.1809
7. SC, 17/24.2.1809
8. SC, 17.2.1809
9. Gould, p.579

Chapter 1

1. Cragg, p.237
2. Healey, p.14
3. DAR 227.5:12
4. King-Hele, pp90-96
5. Healey, p.17
6. DAR 227.5:7

7. DAR 227.5:7
8. DAR 227.5:12
9. Anna Seward, quoted in King-Hele, p.213
10. Oswald, Philip, 'Charles Darwin, The Shropshire Years', *Shropshire Conservation Trust Bulletin*, 53, 1982, SA BD 22 v.f.
11. King-Hele, p.213
12. Ibid
13. Account Book 1790-1815, p.23, DAR 225.5:38
14. Porter and Porter, pp119-120
15. *Autobiography*, Penguin edition, p.11
16. SC 20.9.1788
17. Pattison, Andrew, 'Thomas Telford's Shrewsbury Team', *Journal of the Railway and Canal Historical Society*, November 2007, pp664-675
18. *Autobiography,* Penguin Edition, p.11
19. *New Experiments on the Ocular Spectra of Light and Colours*, by Robert Waring Darwin, MD, read at the Royal Society 23 March 1786. There is a copy in Watton's cuttings, vol. 10, p.232, SA C04 859
20. King-Hele, pp213-4
21. Obituary of Charles Darwin, *Salopian Shreds and Patches*, April 26th 1882, p.40, SA
22. DAR 227.1:129
23. George Peacock, *Life of Thomas Young*, MD, FRS (London, John Murray, 1855). Quoted in British *Medical Journal*, Vol. 335, p.348 (18 August 2007)
24. Porter and Porter, pp81-83. For a Shropshire example, where a duel was only averted by the authorities, see S.A. Watton's cuttings, Vol. 4, p.436
25. Posner, p.51
26. For more information on the Houlstons and William Withering, see booklet entitled *Walking with the Ancestors* at www.wellingtonla21.org.uk/discover
27. King-Hele, p.123
28. King-Hele, pp164-5
29. *Appeal to the Faculty concerning the case of Mrs Houlston*, by R.W. Darwin MD FRS, pub. 7 Feb 1789, SA 665/3/104
30. SC, 17.11.1848
31. SC, 22.7.1791
32. W. Phillips, Shropshire Men, SA Mic. 166, Vol. 4, p.13ff
33. SC 11.10.1788
34. See, for example, the appointment of Thomas DuGard in 1811, SC 15 & 22.3.1811
35. For a history of the first 100 years of the infirmary, see Bevan; Howie discusses in detail how it was administered
36. Bevan, table 8, records the diagnoses and employment of 1,059 inpatients in the year 1845/6
37. Downes, p.2

Chapter 2

1. King-Hele, p.213
2. King-Hele, p.255
3. RW Darwin account book 1790-1815, DAR227.5:38, p.4
4. Ibid., p.5
5. Skempton, A.W. et al, *A Biographical Dictionary of Civil Engineers in Great Britain and Ireland*, Vol. 1 1500-1830, appendix 1, p.828 (Thomas Telford Ltd – Institute of Civil Engineers, 2002)
6. SC 4.2.1791
7. St Chad's Trustees' minute books, 4.2.1791 & 14.7.1791, SA 1048/63 (253/J/1/5)
8. SA D3651/E/1/1/15-16
9. SA D3651/E/3/1/1/18
10. DAR 227.5:38, p.14

11. *Autobiography*, Penguin Edition, p.19
12. Trinder, 1983, p.70
13. Bellamy, pp92ff
14. Plymley, Joseph, *A General View of the Agriculture of Shropshire*, B. McMillan, London (1801) SA
15. Ibid., pp73,78
16. 'A Few Recollections of Dr Darwin', SC 7.2.1902, p.3
17. King-Hele, pp231-2
18. SC 22.4.1791
19. SC 8.7.1791
20. SC 22.7.1791
21. See Katherine Plymley's diaries, SA 1066/1ff; also www.bbc.co.uk/shropshire/content/articles/2007/03/01/slavery_plymley_diaries
22. www.royalhumanesociety.org.uk
23. SC 4.3.1791
24. SC 18.3.1791
25. SC 10.6.1791
26. Eddowes *Shrewsbury Journal*, 31.5.1848
27. King-Hele, p.303
28. Healey, p.10
29. Ibid., pp24-26
30. Wedgwood and Wedgwood, p.74
31. Healey, p.18
32. Woodall, RD
33. Ibid., p.39
34. King-Hele, p.301

Chapter 3

1. Quoted in DeSaulles, p.83
2. Eyton family correspondence, SA 665/6032
3. DAR 227.9:30
4. DAR 227.9:31
5. SA D3651/E/3/1/1/17
6. DAR 227.1:160
7. Alcock, p.10
8. Details from 1866 sale catalogue, SA 552/30/332
9. For more information see Garner, and Morriss and Hoverd
10. Hobbs, p.17
11. DCP, letter 200, March 1833
12. SA 4791/1/3, p.424
13. Philips, W., p.13ff
14. DAR 227.5:38, pp34-5
15. www.peterboyd.com/darwingard3.htm
16. Browne, p.17
17. DAR 227.5:30
18. Shropshire Archives
19. SC 13.11.1846 records the death of Edward Evans 'for upwards of 30 years faithful servant of Dr Darwin of this town.'
20. DCP, letter 4690, 1.12.1864
21. DCP letter 610, 18.10.1841
22. DAR 227.5:38, pp34-5
23. Healey, p.58
24. *Autobiography*, Thinker's Library Edition, p.3, footnote

25. Healey, p.181
26. SA 552/30/333
27. Healey, p.59
28. *Salopian Shreds and Patches*, 6 Sept 1882, p.87, SA
29. SA D3651/E/3/1/1/17 details that part of the settlement relevant to Shrewsbury
30. SA D3651/D/46/1/92
31. DAR 227.5:38, pp34-35
32. See, for example Desmond and Moore, pp12ff, Hubble, pp77ff
33. King-Hele, pp324-328
34. Ibid., p.327
35. Lichfield Library, D262/1/33-34
36. Qualified as an apothecary and surgeon, Dr DuGard had been house surgeon to the Salop Infirmary (Bevan, unpaginated). He then bought an MD degree from the University of Aberdeen for 'the usual fee' (see 'The Trial of Mr Nice', *The British Annals of Medicine*, Vol. 1, pp438-442, quoted in Richard Moore, 'The Spirited Surgeons of Shropshire – Purblind or Visionary', unpublished essay). After this he went into practice in the town as a physician, and was elected physician to the Salop Infirmary in 1811, a position he held till just before his death (SC 29.3.1811; 3.1.1840; St Mary's Church burial record 2247). For an assessment of Dr DuGard's character see Edward Woodall, p.10
37. Healey, p.60
38. Robert Darwin's expenses book (DAR 227.5:38, p.45) notes that Dr DuGard was paid £100 on 6 Feb 1805 on Thomas Wedgwood's account (which the Darwins were administering), which must have been his fee for this consultation. The entry is in Susannah's writing, not Robert's

Chapter 4

1. Erasmus was often called 'Eras' by his family. I have followed this name when there is confusion with his grandfather or uncle of the same name, but have mostly called him by his full name
2. Broadbent, pp2-4
3. Ibid., p.12
4. *Autobiography*, Penguin Edition, p.55
5. SA f.c. 59.6
6. Details of these records are in the copies of the registers in Shropshire Archives
7. King-Hele, p.320
8. Confusingly, Catherine was christened Catherine Emily at St Chad's Church, but thereafter always appears as Emily Catherine in official documents, such as Robert Darwin's will. However, she was always known as Catherine, or Catty, among the family
9. Healey, pp57-8
10. Wedgwood and Wedgwood, p.124
11. Browne, p.18
12. Desmond and Moore, p.12
13. Wedgwood and Wedgwood, p.125
14. Healey, p.67
15. Desmond and Moore, p.12
16. Hubble, p.77
17. Ibid., p.79
18. King-Hele, p.61
19. www.kirjasto.sci.fi.rousse.htm
20. *Autobiography*, Penguin Edition, p.18
21. Browne, p.11
22. *Autobiography*, Penguin edition, p.1
23. Wedgwood and Wedgwood, pp174-6
24. Hubble, p.78
25. DAR 112:117

26. Browne, p.16
27. *Autobiography*, Thinkers' Library Edition, p.4
28. Ibid., p.5, footnote
29. St Chad's Church burial record, SA P.253, fiche 30
30. Quoted in Browne, p.19
31. Parkes, D, SA 6001/3060, p.37
32. *Autobiography*, Penguin edition, p.6
33. Ibid.
34. Ibid., p.2

Chapter 5

1. Desmond and Moore, p.14
2. DCP, Letter 1, 4.1.1822
3. Bessy Wedgwood to Sally Allen, 15.12.1824, quoted in Quinn, p.21
4. Wedgwood and Wedgwood, p.195
5. Caroline to Charles, 22.3.1826, quoted in Boyd, p.5
6. *Autobiography*, Penguin Edition, p.7
7. Ibid., p.19-20
8. Oldham, p.86
9. Desmond and Moore, p.14
10. *Autobiography*, Penguin Edition, p.8
11. Browne, p.23ff
12. Fisher, p.293
13. Browne, p.28
14. Fisher, p.274-5
15. Fisher, p.319ff; Quinn, p.10
16. Fisher, p.315
17. *Autobiography*, Penguin Edition, p.10
18. Woodall, Edward, p.16
19. 'A Second Letter to Henry Bangham, Esq, MP … ' by Samuel Butler DD FAS, headmaster of Shrewsbury School, Eddowes Printer 1821, SA 665/3/137
20. *Autobiography*, Penguin Edition, p.22; Quinn, p.8 provides the translation
21. Healey, p.79
22. Lerwill, C., *The Darwins of Shrewsbury*, undated leaflet, SA VF BD22
23. Bessy Wedgwood to Sally Allen, quoted in Quinn, p.21
24. Meteyard, p.265
25. Millington's Hospital Trustees minutes book SA 2133/12, 10.4.1833
26. Obituary of Robert Darwin – *Shrewsbury Chronicle*, 17.11.1848
27. Lerwill, p.1
28. www.infed.org/thinkers/et-pest.htm
29. Lerwill, p.1 – I have not been able to trace the source of this quotation, and if the date is correct it must refer to the twenty-fifth anniversary of the school, not the twentieth as the writer states
30. *Quarterly Review*, September 1842, quoted by Fisher, p.306
31. Quoted in Oldham, p.77
32. Revd W.G. Humphry, quoted in Fisher, p.305

Chapter 6

1. *Autobiography*, Penguin Edition, p.11
2. *Salopian Shreds and Patches* (SSP), Vol.V, p.87
3. SSP, Vol.V, p.164
4. SSP, Vol.V, p.87
5. Lilian Haywood, SC, 27.11.1959

6. Quinn, p.23
7. Anna Seward, quoted in Healey, p.213
8. *Autobiography*, Penguin Edition, p.11
9. This is still the upper limit for many scales today, so when weighing people over twenty-four stone in the surgery I have had to resort to using two sets of scales, balancing one foot on each
10. Phillips
11. SSP, Vol.V, p.164
12. *Notes and Queries*, SC, 24.11.1902, p.3
13. Quinn, p.23
14. *Notes and Queries*, SC, 7.2.1902, p.3
15. Millington's Hospital Trustees' minute book, 17.1.1807, SA 2133/12
16. Quinn, p.22
17. DCP, letter 74, 3.11.1829
18. Bevan, unpaginated

Chapter 7

1. Meteyard, p.360
2. Information on the Parker family is from DCP – www.darwinproject.ac.uk/darwinletters/namedefs/ but Dr Henry Parker's date of death is wrong. The correct date is from his gravestone. Phillips gives different dates of birth and qualification
3. SA St Chad's register fiche 253/53, entry 186
4. DCP, letter 18, 4.12.1825
5. DCP, letter 288, 22.11.1835
6. Wedgwood and Wedgwood, p.196
7. SC 18.9.1846
8. Meteyard, p.360
9. Ibid., p.265
10. SA 6001/134, p.40, [?] = illegible word
11. DAR 227.5:67
12. Birmingham City Archives, Galton papers MS 3101/C/D/10/1/6
13. Ibid., MS 3101/C/D/10/6/136
14. Herefordshire Record Office, Pateshall Family of Allensmore records A95/V/G/81-104; 136-232
15. Meteyard, p.359
16. Meteyard, pp202-3
17. Susannah Darwin to Josiah Wedgwood, March 29th, 1808, quoted in Meteyard, p.359
18. Hill family archives SA 811/65
19. Woodall, E., pp14-15
20. Meteyard, p.264
21. Ibid., p.265
22. SC 7.2.1902, p.3
23. *Salopian Shreds and Patches*, 1882-3, p.87, SA
24. Wedgwood and Wedgwood, pp190-1
25. Sarah Wedgwood to Josiah Wedgwood, August 1823

Chapter 8

1. *Autobiography*, Penguin Edition, p.11
2. Bevan, table 8, unpaginated
3. *Autobiography*, Penguin Edition, p.15
4. DAR 227.5:141
5. *Autobiography*, Penguin Edition, pp18-19
6. SC 23.8.1788 has an advert from the Montgomery doctors for an assistant who needed to be a man-midwife

7. DAR 227.5:141
8. Eyton family papers, SA 665/6033
9. *Autobiography*, Penguin Edition, p.18
10. Ibid.
11. *Autobiography*, Penguin Edition, p.17
12. 'A Few Recollections of Dr Darwin,' part 1, SC 24.1.1902, p.3
13. Ibid
14. *Autobiography*, Penguin Edition, p.18
15. Des Spence, *British Medical Journal*, vol.335, p.1158 (1.12.2007)
16. *Autobiography*, Penguin Edition, p.16
17. Ibid., p.17
18. Woodall, E., pp9-10
19. Quoted in Browne, p.17
20. Phillips, *Shropshire Men*, SA Mic. 166, Vol. 4, 200-202. Robert Darwin was friendly with the younger Robert Pemberton (DAR 227.6:491)
21. *Autobiography*, Penguin Edition, p.17
22. Matthew Davidson file, copy lodged at Ironbridge Gorge Museum Library, 12.3.1801
23. Royle, p.2
24. DAR 227.5:141 (unless stated, all references to Robert Darwin's treatments come from this source)
25. Porter and Porter, pp157-8
26. Ibid., p.51
27. Eyton family records, SA 665/6033
28. 'A Few Recollections of Dr Darwin,' part 2, SC 7.2.1902, p.3
29. Royle, p.206
30. Eyton family records, SA 665/6033, one word is illegible
31. SA 1781/6/68
32. *Autobiography*, Penguin Edition, p.16
33. Eyton family records, SA 665/5975, 28.7.1802
34. Quoted by Theodore Dalrymple, *British Medical Journal*, vol. 335, p.941 (3 November 2007)

Chapter 9

1. Notebooks lent by the Hazledine family to the author
2. SA D3651/D/46/1/92-94
3. DAR 227.5:31
4. DAR 227.5:36
5. Wedgwood and Wedgwood, p.136
6. Figures from DAR 227.5:38
7. Skempton, A.W., and Johnson, H.R., 'The First Iron Frames', *Architectural Review*, March 1962, p.179
8. Wedgwood and Wedgwood, p.132
9. Ibid., pp172-3
10. DAR 227.5:38, pp12-13
11. Ibid., p.22
12. Childe family records, SA 1045/908
13. Glynne Mytton collection, SA 3766/2/1/1-204
14. www.gtj.org.uk/en/item10/25203
15. SA 3766/2/2/67
16. SC Jan 1829 – the advertisements cost £5 6s 3d
17. SA 3766/2/1/73; Powys County Archives, Garth Estate Record Books M/D/GA/1/1
18. Ibid., M/D/GA/1/2-3
19. Ibid., M/D/GA/1/5
20. Browne, p.8
21. SC 7.2.1903, p.3

22. *Autobiography*, Penguin edition, p.19
23. For example, he gave 10s 6d to a charity for prison relief in 1822 (SC 2.8.1822), and £100 towards the building of the new hospital in 1830 (Bevan, unpaginated)

Chapter 10

1. *Autobiography*, Penguin Edition, p.23
2. DCP, letter 201, 7.3.1833
3. DCP, letter 18, 4.12.1825
4. DCP, letter 19, 2.1.1826
5. DCP, letter 31, 11.4.1826
6. DCP, letter 29, 27.3.1826
7. DCP, letter 31, 11.4.1826
8. *Autobiography*, Penguin Edition, pp26-28
9. DCP, letter 41, 30.3.1828
10. Quoted in Hubble, p.78
11. DCP, letter 19, 2.1.1826
12. Quoted in Browne, p.16
13. Ibid
14. Hubble, p.78
15. DCP, letter 41, 30.3.1828
16. DCP, letter 100, 11.5.1831
17. *Autobiography*, Penguin Edition, p.34
18. Wedgwood and Wedgwood, p.214
19. *Autobiography*, Penguin Edition, p.29
20. DCP, letter 290, 28.12.1835
21. *Autobiography*, Penguin Edition, p.39
22. Ibid.
23. DCP, letter 108, 30th August 1831
24. DCP, letter 109, 31st August 1831 – Josiah Wedgwood's enclosure letter is DCP 110
25. DCP, letter 111, 1st September 1831
26. Gould, p.578
27. Browne, Introduction, p.xi
28. Ibid., p.xii
29. *Autobiography*, Penguin Edition, p.39

Chapter 11

1. DCP, letter 160, 12.2.1832
2. DCP, letter 233, 3.12.1833
3. Ibid.
4. DCP, letter 170, 12.5.1832
5. DCP, letter 201, 7.3.1833
6. DCP, letter 170, 12.5.1832
7. DCP, letter 288, 22.11.1835
8. DCP, letter 253, 9.8.1834
9. DCP, letter 225, 29.10.1833
10. DCP, letter 224, 28.10.1833
11. DCP, letter 237, 12.2.1834
12. DCP, letter 411, May 1838
13. DCP, letter 224, 28.10.1833
14. See, for example, Browne, photos after p.176
15. Wedgwood, Martin, 'Two Wedgwood Family Portraits: A Mystery Solved?' *Ars Ceramica*, 1996, pp54-57

16. National Library of Wales, Aston Hall Correspondence (3), 4735
17. DCP, letter 160, 12.2.1832
18. DCP, letter 170, 12.5.1832
19. DCP, letter 180, 15.8.1832
20. DCP, letter 200, 3.3.1833
21. DCP, letter 201, 7.3.1833
22. DCP, letter 219, 15.10.1833
23. DCP, letter 237, 12.2.1834
24. DCP, letter 268, 16.2.1835
25. DCP, letter 288, 22.11.1835
26. DCP, letter 206, 22.5.1833
27. Annual report of the Salop Infirmary, midsummer 1831, SA 3909/6/2
28. DCP, letter 180, 15.8.1832
29. DCP, letter 191, 12.11.1832
30. Ibid.
31. DCP, letter 208, 29.5.1833
32. DCP, letter 219, 15.10.1833
33. DCP, letter 224, 28.10.1833
34. DCP, letter 246, 23.5.1834
35. DCP, letter 160, 12.2.1832
36. DCP, letter 201, 7.3.1833. A full account of the gardens and plants at The Mount is in Boyd, 2006, pp5ff
37. DCP, letter 160, 12.2.1832
38. DCP, letter 542, 27.10.1839
39. DCP, letter 180, 15.8.1832
40. DCP, letter 208, 29.5.1833
41. Wedgwood and Wedgwood, pp261-2
42. DCP, letter 297, 12.2.1836
43. C. Darwin to W.D. Fox, 7.6.1837, quoted in Wedgwood and Wedgwood, p.228
44. Wedgwood and Wedgwood, p.228
45. DAR 227.6:405, 30.6.1837
46. St George's Church, SA fiche 254/6
47. DAR 265:9
48. DCP, letter 438, 15.11.1838
49. DCP, letter 431, 11.11.1838
50. DCP, letter 433, 13.11.1838
51. DCP, letter 438, 15.11.1838
52. Healey, p.2
53. SA D3651/D/23/298
54. Wedgwood and Wedgwood, p.238; DAR 265:9
55. DCP, letter 621, 22.2.1842
56. DCP, letter 623, 13.3.1842

Chapter 12

1. DAR 265:9
2. DCP, letter 801, 20.12.1844; letter 833, ?Nov 1844
3. DCP, letter 719, 2.12.1843
4. Details from DAR 265:9
5. Some of these loans are detailed in SA – Salt Collection D3651/B/1/2/87,/93,/99,/109; 552/7/605 (Earls of Powis); D3651/B/2/2/11 (Walcots); D3651/B/33/4/37,50,57 (Humffreys); Attingham Collection 112/5/14/22-28, 112/5/19/12,23,27,28,56-7; Glynne Mytton Collection 3766/2/4/330; Kinlet Collection SRO 1945/908

6. DCP, letter 980, 27.5.1846
7. DCP, letters 673 (27.4.1843), 674 (8.12.1843), 719 (2.12.1843), 766 (25.7.1844)
8. Browne, p.551
9. Ibid., p.9
10. DCP letter 801, 20.12.1844
11. DAR 265:9
12. DCP, letter 1179, 25.5.1848
13. DCP, letter 1206, 12.11.1848
14. DCP, 1207, 13.11.1848
15. SC, 17.11.1848
16. Wedgwood and Wedgwood, pp249-250
17. Copy of the Will from the Public Record Office, proved 19 December 1848
18. Ibid, p.2
19. Browne, p.9
20. See Glynne-Mytton papers, SA 3766/2/4/330; Kinlet collection, SA 1045/368; 1045/908-909
21. DCP, letter 1211, 6.12.1848
22. DCP, letter 1222, 6.2.1849
23. DCP, letter 1234, 19.3.1849
24. DCP, letter 1236, 28.3.1849

Chapter 13

1. Healey, pp202ff
2. Ibid., p.205
3. *Autobiography*, Thinker's Library Edition, Appendix I, pp106-8
4. DCP, letter 1416, 25.4.1851
5. DCP, letter 1420, 25.4.1851
6. DCP, letter 1421, 25.4.1851
7. DCP, letter 1423, 27.4.1851
8. Wedgwood and Wedgwood, p.263
9. DCP, letter 623, 13.3.1842
10. Wedgwood and Wedgwood, p.263
11. DCP, letter 1568, 1.5.1854
12. Wedgwood and Wedgwood, p.280
13. DCP, letter 2538, after 21.11.1859
14. DCP, letter 2545, 23.11.1859
15. SA BD 22 v.f. 8068/1 [SC/1/81]
16. Julia Wedgwood to Effie Wedgwood, quoted in Wedgwood and Wedgwood, p.273
17. Details of Catherine and Charles Langton are in Wedgwood and Wedgwood, pp217, 220, 240-1, 246 and 272-3
18. DCP, letter 4968, January 1866, footnote 3
19. Wedgwood and Wedgwood, p.272
20. The death certificate reads, 'scirrhous disease of the cervical glands', which in modern language is 'hard and enlarged glands of the neck', most likely resulting from cancer of some sort
21. DCP, letter 4968, January 1866
22. The date of death is from the death certificate. Eddowes *Shrewsbury Journal* 7.2.1866 records the date as 2 February
23. Wedgwood and Wedgwood, p.329
24. DCP, letter 5010, 19.2.1866
25. DCP, letter 4924, October 1865
26. Millington's Hospital Trustees' minute books, SA 2133/14, 16.12.1865
27. Ibid., 2.2.1866
28. Alcock, p.41

29. The death certificate reads 'exhaustion due to long continued uterine disease', which presumably means bleeding, which, if it occurs after the menopause, would be most likely due to cancer
30. DCP, letter 5217, 25.9.1866
31. Information from death certificate and census records, 1841-1861
32. Wedgwood and Wedgwood, p.288
33. Miscellaneous Letters in Shropshire and North Wales Natural History and Antiquarian Society SA 6001/134, p.49
34. DCP, letter 5230, 4.10.1866
35. DCP, letters 5233 & 5238, 7&11.10.1866
36. DCP, letter 5238
37. DCP, letter 5230, 4.10.1866
38. DCP, letter 5238
39. Wedgwood and Wedgwood, p.288
40. Sale Catalogue for the contents of the Mount, SA BD 22 v.f. 8068/1
41. www.peterboyd.com/darwingard3.htm
42. Wedgwood and Wedgwood, p.288
43. www.peterboyd.com/darwingard3.htm
44. DCP, letters 5369 and 5428, 17.7.1867, 3.3.1867
45. G.P.B. Whitwell, 'Charles Darwin's own Evolution in Shrewsbury, Market Drayton and around the Breiddons' [sic], *Shropshire Magazine*, July 1950, p.44
46. Quoted in www.peterboyd.com/darwingard3.htm
47. Eddowes *Shrewsbury Journal*, 10.10.1866
48. W. Phillips, *Shropshire Men*, SA Mic 166, Vol. 4, p.13ff

Epilogue
1. Hubble, p.77
2. Healey, p.315
3. Wedgwood and Wedgwood, p.305; Healey, pp291-2
4. Wedgwood and Wedgwood, p.324
5. Ibid., p.305
6. Healey, pp307-8
7. Ibid.
8. Ibid., p.316
9. Wedgwood and Wedgwood, pp316-8
10. Ibid., p.318
11. Healey, p.319-22
12. For example, Woodall, E., in 1885
13. *Autobiography*, Thinker's Library Edition, p.2
14. DAR 112:117
15. *Autobiography*, Thinker's Library Edition, p.7
16. Caroline Wedgwood to Emma Darwin, 19th November 1887, cited in Wedgwood and Wedgwood, p.326
17. Graber, R.B., and Miles, L.P., 'In Defence of Darwin's Father', *History of Science* xxvi, pp97-102 (1988)
18. Healey, p.308
19. Wedgwood and Wedgwood, p.344

INDEX

Other titles published by The History Press

Haunted Shrewsbury

MARTIN WOOD

From heart-stopping accounts of poltergeists to first-hand encounters with ghouls, this book will appeal to anyone who wants to know more about Shrewsbury's mysterious history. Drawing on historical and contemporary sources, this collection of tales contains a chilling range of ghostly goings-on. Discover the headless apparition at the castle gates, ghostly monks from the abbey church and a whole family of spirits in Milk Street. The phenomenal gathering of spooks in Shrewsbury will captivate anyone interested in the supernatural history of the area.

978 0 7524 4303 4

Crime and Punishment: Shrewsbury

MARTIN WOOD

'You shall be taken from this place hence to a place of execution, and may God have mercy on your soul'. With these words many a person has been sent to their death by the hands of an executioner. This light-hearted yet well-researched exploration of punishments in Shrewsbury over the centuries features tales of criminals and their misdeeds, from the Romans to the last execution to take place in Shrewsbury in 1960. Stories of Shrewsbury's criminals, such as Thomas Hughes, who was whipped for stealing a turkey, are bound to captivate anyone interested in Shrewsbury's more shadowy history.

978 0 7524 4546 5

Breweries & Bottlers of Wellington

ALLAN FROST

Mention breweries and pop works in Wellington and almost everyone will remember the Murphy family who owned The Wrekin Brewery and O.D. Murphy's Wrekin Mineral Water Works for some fifty years. But that's only half the story. Lavishly illustrated with plans, memorabilia and many previously unpublished photographs, this is the definitive history of brewing and bottling in the historic medieval market town of Wellington in Shropshire.

978 0 7524 4631 8

Around Shrewsbury: Volume II

DEREK WALLEY

Part of the Images of England series, and filled with previously unseen and rare pictures and photographs, this book is guaranteed to bring back nostalgic memories to those who have lived in Shrewsbury, and provide an insight into the town's history for those new to the area. A must-read for residents and newcomers alike.

978 0 7524 3371 4